W9-BAS-799

CAREERS
AF!

M. Michelle Nadon

 FriesenPress

Suite 300 - 990 Fort St
Victoria, BC, V8V 3K2
Canada

www.friesenpress.com

ISBN
978-1-5255-4111-7 (Hardcover)
978-1-5255-4112-4 (Paperback)
978-1-5255-4113-1 (eBook)

1. BUSINESS & ECONOMICS, CAREERS, JOB HUNTING

Distributed to the trade by The Ingram Book Company

Special discounts can be made available for bulk purchases; large quantities can be arranged as sales promotions, or for corporate use with corporate logos. Send an email request to: nadon@mediaintelligence.ca

TABLE OF CONTENTS

Dedicated to Mary Dwyer-Nadon
"Parliament-Girl Extraordinaire"

INTRODUCTION

"I'VE GOT TO GET OUT OF THIS TOWN, IT'S JUST NO GOOD FOR ME."

I was sixteen years old when I wrote that in one of my journals, back in 1976. I didn't know it then, but as I look back, it's clear that "career-activism" is coded in my DNA.

I was raised in a government town in a working-class family. When we grew up, we were expected to get a (any) job and (largely) stay in it for life. Personal happiness and professional fulfillment were not part of the regular discourse. Yet even at that tender age, I *instinctively* knew that I wanted and needed a much bigger world.

As with most industry newcomers, my twenties were all about experimentation and survival. I didn't give much thought at all to my future. At the time, it was all about moving to Toronto and dealing with "right now".

"Right now" proved to be an intensely difficult decade. In each of the series of less-than-compelling jobs I ended up in, I found myself always daydreaming about what it was that I would really like to do—not just what I thought I had to do. When I stumbled into the arts and cultural arena in my late twenties, I finally found what I had needed all along: *work that spoke directly to my heart.*

I was incredibly eager to learn, and during my thirties I was as ambitious as all get out. When I saw a job I wanted, I went for it. I was never shy to take on something I hadn't done before.

I came to learn (curiously) that *motivation follows action.* Most people wait for motivation to strike before acting. But I had always been motivated by "taking action." And it wasn't so much about the moves I was making, as *it was about the thinking behind the moves.* Each job I took on, I would ask myself: "What do I want next? Where do I want to be five years from now? What do I need to do to get it?

My "M.O." was learning! Professional development. University courses. Events. Conferences. Volunteering. Committees. Networking. I tried my hand at writing editorials, public speaking, as well as developing and delivering curriculum. I tracked media stakeholders and companies in a giant "contacts database." I read industry forecasts, business trends, and everything I could get my hands on regarding business best practices.

By my forties, I had broken into the senior ranks and had developed some executive chops, as well as some professional standing. I began to see how many of my colleagues were actually held back because they were so good at their jobs. I also witnessed colleagues' lives beginning to be hugely disrupted by the growing "gig economy." *I came to understand that it's not just about "who you know," it was more about "how you worked it."* So . . . I learned to work it. Each step of the way, I grew my skills and knowledge, and learned how to better position myself, how to better leverage my growing networks, and how to keep the concept of "career activism" at the forefront of all my professional activities.

Mid-career, I hit the ceiling, as well as the curb. By then, I was too senior for mid-management jobs. Without greater educational credentials, I wasn't going to enjoy more upward mobility. And, I wasn't alone—I found both male and female peers equally and similarly challenged with "horizontal mobility", and its evil counterpart "under-employment" as their only options. Then, my latest contract expired with no continuance on offer. (Insert giant sigh.)

I had, by then, also thankfully learned that I could probably generate income if I could figure out a way to fix a business problem. In this case, I saw clear improvements that could be made with respect to my industry's hiring practices. And a light bulb went off! I thought: "What if I could start a company that would address the needs of both the employer as well as the talent?" Hm . . . And I wondered: *"Did I have enough nerve to start my own business?"* Was it even plausible?

After a year's worth of market research (and a solid kick over the finish line from an industry exec who had my best interests at heart), I launched a small recruiting firm—one that would equitably source and screen talent for my industry, while also placing a strong focus on the talent's career aspirations and ambitions.

Fifteen years of recruiting and thousands of career-coaching sessions later, I've never looked back. Each year, I ask myself the hard questions about what I want next, and I challenge myself to be willing to do what I need to do, to get it. *In short, I continue to take the time it takes to get ahead of the process, rather than be victim to it.*

"Career activism" has indeed become a way of life.

And it has served me exceptionally well.

> **"** *You don't need to know exactly what you want to do. That first position after graduation isn't a destination—it's just the next step in your journey. It's normal to move through a variety of sectors in the course of your career. For the most part, you're looking at a discovery journey. Focus on the key strengths that you can build, and are building, through the course of a lifetime.* **"**
>
> —Caroline Konrad, director, Career & Co-op Centre
> **www.ryerson.ca**

My goal in writing this book is not so much to offer up a "career drunkalogue" (LOL), as it is to encourage others to follow my lead by getting clear on what it is that they want out of life—whether you start in your twenties, your thirties, your forties, your fifties, or even your sixties! It is to encourage all job seekers and freelancers to take risks on themselves. It is also to de-mystify the hiring process by offering practical strategies to help manage career moves with confidence—at the right times, and for the right reasons. My aim is to empower talent to make stronger, more targeted decisions about their career moves, and encourage them to take the necessary steps toward voicing and realizing their goals.

Because . . . if I can (and did) do it, anyone can. At the end of the day, *it is not so much about "my story", as it is about the concerted path I charted for myself*—a path that you can undoubtedly chart for yourself too.

My plan for my sixties is to continue to provide career coaching and customized agenting services for talent, while I turn my sights towards writing two or three non-fiction books on my passion projects: animal rescue and animal advocacy. And, as I roll out my plan for this next, truly exciting phase of my professional career, there are three critical things that I want to impart:

Thing 1: Stop. Get quiet. Listen to both your heart and your gut. Forget about new years' resolutions, or wishing and hoping, and instead, challenge yourself to **make a bold, new "happy birthday wish list", each and every year of your precious life**. Stop, get centered, and listen to your instincts, as well as your heart. Make the time to get clear on what it is that you actually want to do, *not what others think you might, or should, or could, do.*

Thing 2: Do not for a single second, think that any one thing cannot be done. Absolutely anything is possible—it doesn't matter what age or stage you are at. Just start: Get in front of it, and seek out communities of interest who share similar professional pursuits. It's all.so.do-able.

Thing 3: Take risks and invest in yourself. Be polite and be prepared, but make your ask! Go meet that person you really want to meet. Invite the chat that you want to have. Ask questions. Get informed. Grow your business knowledge and business acumen. Be present. Stake your claim. Ask for help, and accept help when it's offered. Go "backstage": find your peeps and hang with them. Sign up for that course, or apply for that program. Write that grant application, or the burning "outreach" email you feel compelled to send. While you're at it, for heaven's sakes, lighten up and let yourself have some fun with it!

★ In other words (and as they say in twelve step programs), "don't be the person who, while dying, has someone else's life flash in front of their eyes." You deserve happiness and fulfillment—it's your birthright. You owe it to your best self to get to know your needs, to own your wants, and to take them out into the world.

Ask yourself on a scale of one to ten: "How well am I managing my career?" "How happy am I, doing what I'm doing?" If your answer is anything less than ten out of ten, read on.

> *There's room to make mistakes early in your career. Go for it, and get them over with early. Pursue your passion; don't worry about income too much. Try different things. Start your own business on the fly—even if it falls on its face and fails, you tried, and you'll learn valuable lessons from the experience.*
>
> —Mark Prasuhn, president
> **www.cmucollege.com**

CHAPTER 1

CAREERS: YOU CAN'T KNOW WHAT YOU DON'T KNOW

The problem with careers is that there are three operatives that are working against you that you probably aren't aware of, or haven't given much thought to.

First, there is the "scarcity principle". Everyone covets jobs and covets intel about jobs, all inside a mindset that will have you believe there is never enough to go around—aka the cup is half empty. The flip side, of course, is a mindset that believes in the "abundance principle", in which the world is full of fantastic resources and there is a place for everyone in it—aka the cup is half full. What this means is that we typically come from a place where, if one person gets ahead, it tends to automatically make another think they are not doing as well. As in: "If you get this, then I won't." It is part of the human condition—and it's socially schooled into us.

The second operative is that the entire hiring and recruiting arena is rife with "power games" and/or "secrecy." There is less qualitative information shared about strategic career management than almost any other topic on earth. Check your social media if you think that might not be true. Almost everything about career mobility is treated in a secretive fashion. As a rule, people don't share job postings and/or information about job opportunities. And it's uncool to share how down and out you are. When it comes to your career, there is seemingly no one and nowhere to turn to, to get specific, individualized help with job leads. It's almost like everyone's actually afraid to share openly about careers.

The final operative: When someone is involved in a hire, they're in a "position of power"—*or so they think.* This puts the job seeker in the "position of not having power"—*or so they think!*

These operatives are what I call the "set ups for failure in job search."

Then, there are the mistakes that you don't even know you're making with respect to your career. I have been asked countless times in my recruiting life: "What are the biggest mistakes a person can make with their career?"

Let's start with the "five biggies."

Mistake #1: A career is not something you take care of only when you're in trouble and your back is against a wall. Rather than attend to their career path and marketing tools on a consistent basis, job seekers tend to use an *ad-hoc, incremental, reactive approach* to job search. They don't understand that they need to proactively nurture their networks and leads in a systematic, ongoing way. And they don't know (read: have never been taught) to pro-actively keep all their marketing tools current (resume, business card, cover letters, social media profiles, e-signatures on emails, references, bio, etc.), let alone to upgrade them on an annual basis. Career management is like getting a tune-up for your car. Tending mindfully to your career is basic, 100% necessary maintenance. You know what happens when you don't schedule that critical tune-up for your car, right? Well, the same principle applies to your career. Regular maintenance is key.

> **"** People need work coaches to help them get some perspective. Coaching is a service that people just don't understand—it's like having your very own HR department. We all need our own personal coaches. **"**
>
> —Jacqueline Nuwame, marketing director
> **www.earin.com**

Mistake #2: Job seekers tend not to do thorough background research on job leads and companies. As a result, they end up in work situations that are . . . well . . . less than stellar, shall we say. Or they end up in jobs that have no hope of actually furthering their careers, which only serve to pay the bills.

> **"** I've had a few amazing jobs, and a few not-so-amazing jobs—choosing the right team is critical, in an environment where people want me to succeed. I've learned to not be afraid to leave a company that doesn't have my best interests in mind. **"**
>
> —Kevin O'Keefe, producer/director
> **www.kevinokeefe.tv**

Mistake #3: Job seekers don't take the time to "script" and "rehearse" their approaches to hiring managers. They do low-level preparation only, instead of drilling down and finding out absolutely everything they possibly can on the company concerned. They jump in completely unprepared and under-rehearsed. Simply skimming the surface (like quickly checking a website) results in very little quantitative information, let alone retention. So when it comes time for an interview, only the barest amount of information will come to mind. What little info you have remains in short-term memory only—which is highly unreliable. If you do your research, however, and rehearse out loud and often, the info goes into your long-term memory. Hello, preparedness! Hello, confidence! Hello, recall!

> **❝** *I developed sales as a habit. At its core, it's being able to understand what someone needs, and to match those needs up with what [skills & knowledge] you have to offer. Selling happens every time you talk to someone about your work.* **❞**
>
> —Frank Pulumbarit, managing principal
> **www.fpconsultinggroup.com**

Mistake #4: Job seekers aren't prepared with a "business case" specifically tailored to each potential job lead. In other words, job seekers don't know how to effectively communicate to hiring managers why they would be the best person for a given job. Job seekers tend to throw in the kitchen sink about all their skills and experience, rather than coming in with a targeted message that tells a hiring manager exactly why their company should hire them over someone else.

> **66** *Love the push to research companies: Just to see where I would like to work, know what the work culture is like, using the job search spreadsheet to figure out who to target and why, and how they fit into my goals.* **99**

—Kadon Douglas, communications
& engagement manager
www.wift.com

Mistake #5: Most job seekers are not taught or encouraged to regularly and consistently invest in their own development (read: spend money *and* time)**.** You need to take a leadership role in your own development and life-long learning. You absolutely need a mentor, and/or learning partners. You must participate in your industry, and you must continue to broaden your knowledge and skills on an ongoing basis. While you're at it, you would be well advised to give a business/career coach some serious consideration.

> **66** *The biggest mistake I've seen is to make significant decisions without the wisdom of sound counsel. It is imperative that one surrounds oneself with good advisors; and that among them there be a diversity of voices.* **99**

—Christa Dickenson, executive director
www.telefilm.ca

CHAPTER 2

THE BIG PICTURE: WHERE DO YOU STAND WITH YOUR CAREER?

Every career has a life cycle.

Every company has a life cycle.

Every industry has a life cycle.

It's critical to know where you stand!

Whatever your career plans, you first need to get an understanding of where you stand on the career continuum. Your career is always a "work in progress", and there are definitive checkpoints or timeframes that can help you assess where you fall on that continuum. Ask yourself:

Are you entry level, new market entrant, or a recent grad (1-5 years)?

Are you mid-management (5-10 years)?

Are you senior management (10-15 years)?

Or are you executive level (15-20 years)?

It's always a good practice to know where you stand on the "career arc" so that you can figure out how your skills and experience stack up. It also helps you figure out what level you are aiming for next. Knowing where you stand helps you articulate where you are at to others, so that they can better guide you. And, it also helps you keep your expectations in line with your actual status.

Career progressions take time!

Some important points to consider:

Point 1: To acquire or achieve "subject matter expertise" (SME) in any topic or functional role, **you must spend 10K hours in it.**

Point 2: It is important to get some perspective on your career. If you think about your future realistically, you will come to understand that you will be looking for work (or work opportunities) for the rest of your adult life (read: ouch!) *So it follows that it's really smart to get good at looking for work.* It just makes sense, right?

Point 3: Seldom is anyone ever told (outright) that "things are going to be all right." But they will be. Ask anyone who is reasonably established in an industry and they will tell you that things really do tend to work out over time. This doesn't negate the fact that managing your career is hard. It is! You will have up times, and you will have down times. You will have frightening times, and you will have victorious times. The person who succeeds will be the one who adjusts to and gets comfortable with all of the above—aka the person who learns from their experience and builds coping skills and genuine resilience accordingly.

Job search is a mega life-stressor: It hits you where it hurts the most—right in the centre of your identity.

For the most part, we don't walk into any job-search process with our heads screwed on straight. Typically, we carry within us **unresolved grief** from previous employment/life experiences and losses. We carry **fear** at worst, and uncertainty or **anxiety** at best—due to a lack of positive affirmation for our professional efforts. We lack practical, tried-and-true, ongoing guidance with our careers.

We can also carry societal **shame** for being unemployed—aka social stigma.

We are all subject to making **incorrect assumptions** about how hiring processes roll out, and why we weren't chosen for a given job. We **jump to conclusions** much more often than we fact-check or give the benefit of the doubt. We **spend endless hours speculating** about what's going on with the decision-makers when most times, (frankly) whatever is going on in the hiring department typically has very little to do with us!

We have **unrealistic expectations** and **immediate gratification** needs. We have both **rational and irrational fears**.

Probably the worst thing of all, is a **collective lack of self-esteem** from inadequate/incorrect past conditioning. As a coach, I couldn't tell you how many people have sat across from me in a career-counselling session who were unable to say anything when asked: "What are you really good at?" Or: "What do you bring to the table that no one else does?" And if, *indeed if,* they can come up with something, their answers tend to be couched as (insecure) questions—not statements of facts "Well, I *think* I'm good at . . . " or "Would you say I'm good at . . .?"

When I hear this, I make a point of immediately telling them all the good things I can readily see in them. Like: They present as a professional; they've invested in their own development and should be proud of that; they are open, friendly, funny. They have good manners. Their work experience has been strong. They are intelligent . . . I rattle off this list of attributes that I can clearly see, in the short amount of time they have been with me. And I get them to write those attributes down. Sometimes, they "tear up" because they have simply never been affirmed before. Sometimes, they beam. Most times, they are shocked that a perfect stranger can come up with a *positive, lengthy list of good things about them*, in no time flat. Kind of makes you wonder who they're hanging with, and how the people in their lives are treating them . . .

Compassion is the name of the game! You must learn to practice self-compassion for your own unique individual process, and also develop compassion for others who are simply trying to navigate their professional lives as you are (even that rude person who won't give you the time of day by responding to your outreach). Remember: The more you experience, the more you learn. **Every setback** is designed to provide you with learning opportunities, which **results in greater coping skills**. Recognize that you are human, and that you will make mistakes—and so will others. That's *how* you learn. (In other words: breathe . . . and let others breathe.)

MINDSET ALERT! Career and businesses coaches are there to answer your questions. But if they are really good coaches, they will teach you how to answer your own questions. To this end, always keep in mind that **each of us inherently knows the difference between right and wrong**. Ask yourself: Does this feel right or wrong? And listen to the answer. If something you are doing doesn't feel right (right now, or, doesn't feel right, period), then don't do it. Or stop doing it. **Learn to listen to your gut and honour your inner reaction**—aka your intuition.

Your gut is called the "second brain" for a good reason—if your gut tells you something is off, it is!

Finally, know that you are not alone. These mindset handicaps are both ubiquitous and universal. Everyone experiences some or all of the above at some, or many, points in their career path. You're not crazy and you're not "a loser." You're just human. And the job market really is as tough as you think!

So: Work hard at shutting off the self-deprecating voice in your head, and shutting out the people who undermine your confidence. Put your energy into figuring out where you stand on the arc of your career, and where you're headed next, instead.

Everything will be fine—just hold up your end, and do your career homework.

> ❝ *You've got to give your passion a fighting chance! Going into a career just for stability is always the wrong choice. Even if it isn't practical, do what you're passionate about and the money will follow. Give it a couple of years and see if it leads anywhere. If you do have to abandon it for practical purposes, at least you tried. When people hit their forties and fifties, they really regret not following their bliss.* ❞
>
> —Alisyn Camerota, CNN anchor
>   **www.alisyncamerota.com**
>   **cnn.com/shows/new-day**

CHAPTER 3

THREE EASY STEPS TO CAREER MANAGEMENT

Step 1: Figure out your *goals* in concrete terms.

Step 2: Develop your *self-marketing tools*.

Step 3: Start a *strategic job search*.

In my experience, one of the biggest issues I see when it comes to careers is that people will just not focus and take the time to make a plan. Correction: *make* the time to make a career plan! They work their careers in fits and starts, instead of concertedly working through the steps to manage their brand *and* their message on a consistent basis throughout each and every year of their career. In fairness, most people don't even know they have "career homework" to do. Say what? That's because society will have you believe that careers just happen. (Note: not on my watch—I make my career happen.)

It's simply a matter of learning a new discipline: aka "career activism."

Here's how it's done: We start at the beginning, by **identifying and prioritizing goals** into short-, mid-, and longer-term strands. Then we look at **best practices for building and managing your personal brand** so that you have up-to-date "marketing tools" with which promote yourself. Then we break **job search** into two distinct functions: job-search "research" and job-search "strategy". The more organized your research, the faster and more qualitative will be the results. The trick lies in keeping *sustained attention on your career*, followed by simply doing your homework. Simple as that: A three-step process!

Most people throw stuff at the wall all their professional lives, and hope that something sticks. When you use that approach, your career is actually managing you. You need to turn this around by taking the power back into your own hands and taking steps to pro-actively manage your career. No more avoidance or passivity. No more reactivity. No more knee-jerk moves, or fits and starts. No more feeling defeated before you even begin. You've got a plan to work!

It truly doesn't matter what age or stage you are at. What matters, is that you develop the discipline of working those three steps: Figuring out your goals, building your marketing tools, and orchestrating a meaningful and gainful job search strategy.

★ **Job seekers tend to turn to friends, peers, and/or family for advice.** Don't be this person! Despite having your best interests at heart, these well-meaning folk are not trained to help you self-actualize, and very few of them know about the new employment rules, let alone the new marketing tools. We're looking for you to make more "truly informed" decisions, building your brand and enhancing your messaging, and get moving with confidence into the job market, making concrete decisions as you go—instead of having decisions be made for you. Doesn't that sound like a better approach?

The good news: I may be the only person to ever tell you that careers (read: any and all goals) are absolutely, completely achievable with the right amount of preparation. Personally, I have learned that there is very little that I set my sights on that I can't (and don't) achieve. If I don't succeed in getting what I want, I know that I probably missed a critical piece of my own homework, or blew it when it came to making my business case!

MINDSET ALERT! Please hear me when I say there is more opportunity out there than you can possibly imagine. The world is in a sorry state. There are untold ways and places for you to apply your unique skills, knowledge, and passion. Think about this: If there is a problem in (any) business, it follows that there is a business imperative to be solved, *and* an accompanying job (or role) to be had solving it. That just makes sense, right? And, yes, dammit, you're allowed! Not only are you allowed to participate and shine, your ideas will actually be welcomed (imagine that) because you will be bringing a solution to the table. You will be welcomed because you will have done your homework, and that homework will resonate positively with (read: inspire confidence in) decision-makers. When you're prepared in your approach and you've built a "business case" it just makes sense that you will be taken more seriously. So get serious!

Reality Check: Go to your front door, open it, and look outside. Do you see a problem anywhere? If you do, congratulations! You've just figured out how to create a job (or business) for yourself. Coming up with a viable solution to a particular problem a company or community is experiencing, is something employers and communities of interest will pay money to fix. That is what business is all about!

So, let's get started on Step 1 by writing up a career wish list. Then we'll look at your personal brand, and take it to the next level. Finally, we'll look at how to access the "hidden job market" to help you secure the job of your dreams.

Easy as 1-2-3!

Allons-y!

> ❝ *Be assertive. Those who are more assertive about the work they do and the recognition they want, get ahead faster. Take more risks. Don't stay in a job if you don't see a clear [growth] path in it.* ❞
>
> —Colette Watson, senior vice-president
> **www.rogersmedia.com**

CHAPTER 4

WHAT'S ON YOUR WISH LIST?

Have you ever, in fact, even written up a career wish list?

The first step to creating your own magic is to make a "wish list" of what _you_ want.

In case no one has ever told you, you owe it to your highest self to own what you actually want in life . . . not what you think the world wants of you, and not what your mother or brother-in-law always thought you ought to do. You'll be amazed at what you come up with if you just get focused for an hour or so, and make some notes on what you might like to pursue for the next year (or handful of years) in your life.

Don't waste any more time trying to "think your way through it" or listening to naysayers (including the ones in your head). The trick is to move your career thoughts out of random cycling through your short-term memory into solidified long-term memory. And that is exactly what happens when you _write down your wish list_. Get serious for an hour, listen to your heart and your gut, and write up all the things you want, both professionally and personally. Shoot for a dozen—or a baker's dozen!

All you have to do is to give yourself the time it takes to write your wish list up, and you'll be off to the best start.

Please note that when you write that wish list up, you want to bring some new thinking to the subject. So . . . leave your regular desk and regular thinking behind. Grab your laptop and treat yourself to an inspirational location. A temple? A bar? A park? (Or anything in between.) Gift yourself with an un-pressured hour. Start by jotting some ideas down about what you would really like to do. Because . . . the minute you start writing your goals down, you are on the road to delivering a much more targeted message.

> **"** *Being passive, or pathless, is a big mistake! You can tell when there's no passion and when someone's just going through the motions. It shows!* **"**
>
> —Frank Pulumbarit, managing principal
> **www.fpconsultinggroup.com**

So, let me ask you again: what do you really want?

This goals exercise will help you figure out the career path you want to pursue: www.mediaintelligence.ca/career-goals-exercise/.

Challenge yourself to write up a bunch of statements that reflect your dream job or wishes—things you would really like to do at this particular stage of your professional life. Add in some personal goals. Professional development goals. Life balance goals. Networking goals. Health, nutrition, exercise, and wellness goals. Relationship goals. Spiritual goals. You get the idea! Write up a full twelve statements on things that you want. Something akin to the example below. But, really, anything goes. Just be sure to write full sentences, as in "statements" containing a subject, a verb, *and* an object. If you can figure out the "shiny objects" that you want to pursue, the ensuing best practices will definitely help you get them.

Goals Examples:

- I would like to own a small business, creating [product/ service] for [market].

- I would like to be a [type] of consultant, in [sector].

- I would like to mentor young professionals in [topic].

- I would like financial security by [age].

- I want to build my knowledge by taking [course/webinar].

- I would like to change jobs or my title this year from [x] to [y].

- I would like more work/life balance by doing [x] by [timeline].

- I've always wanted to volunteer for [cause].

- I want to find a qualified specialist to help me with [x issue].

- I want to upgrade my marketing tools and my brand this year.

- I would like to join [association] to build my network.

- Etc.

The sooner you identify your goals, the faster you will start realizing them.

Super bonus: The act of writing down your goals is totally ingenious because it actually *forces you to articulate what you want*. Most people never push themselves to articulate what they want and, as a result, they don't get much of anything. The more you practice writing down your goals, the better you become at expressing them. It just makes sense! The more directly you express your asks, the more targeted the support you will get from your professional community.

MINDSET ALERT! For heaven's sakes, try to have some fun with your goals! If you always wanted to be the prime minister of Canada, write it down. You've always wanted to photograph sea turtles in their natural environments? Write it down. You want financial stability by [x] age? Climb to the top of the corporate ladder in [x] industry? Run your own business doing [x]? You want to get healthier in [x] by [timeframe]? You would like to invest in [extra education/professional development]? Or, you want to increase your soft skills, like networking, empathy, leadership, or just plain have more confidence doing [x]? You get the idea: Write them all down! What's the worst that can happen if you allow yourself to own what you want? Worst case scenario, you will lose an hour of your life. Contrast that with gaining decades of personal happiness and fulfillment!

Pretend, for a little while, that some benevolent rich person has your back, and is willing to write the cheque to make your wish list come true. Wouldn't that be cool? What would you do if someone were to write you that cheque? What have you always wanted that you have thought to be impossible, or, were too afraid to voice? What have you under-sold yourself for, or, gotten talked out of, or, have been dissed or silenced for, or, felt you had to put someone else's needs before your own? Hm? Now imagine the best: getting exactly what you want. *It's simple: you own it, you plan it, and then you earn it.*

You don't have to "settle." Why would you? Who taught you that settling is all that you are allowed? You deserve to be fulfilled . . . Don't you think?

Having trouble writing up your wish list? Try writing up your goals with your *non-dominant hand*. Stay patient, and write down your random thoughts. If you stick with it, you will be amazed at what comes out. The trick to using your non-dominant hand is this: They say that your left and right brains control different types of thinking. So, if your left brain (the analytical side) stalls and won't release the information you're seeking, let your non-dominant hand tease some ideas out of your right brain (the creative side). It's *such a cool thing* to do! (Revelatory, in fact.)

If you follow through on writing up your goals and learn how to crunch them annually (refer to Chapter 5's "How to Take Your Wish List to the Next Level"), you will see changes and greater successes in your career, much faster!

When you take a leadership position on your wants and needs, you'll be off to the strongest start. You'll make your professional reality much more meaningful, gainful and literally, powerful! The simple act of writing down your goals is the first step in delivering a more targeted message. No more waffling, vagueness, or confusion. No more avoidance, generalizations, or denying your own voice. No more playing it safe.

Round one! Ding! Ding! Ding! We have a winner!

> **" "** *Formalizing (writing down) my career plan showed me that my goals were achievable—all that I had to do was to be systematic about pursuing them. I began to see that it is indeed possible to put my dreams into action, by visualizing and organizing them into concrete steps. I see my career now as more of a "series of ongoing tasks."*

—Gloria Ui Young Kim, filmmaker
https://gloriauiyoungkim.wordpress.com/about/

Gloria's got it exactly right.

If you really want to rock your career/life plan, write up a new wish list each year on your birthday. We all grow and change. We evolve—as do our wants and needs. Do with your wish list what you will—it's *your* list! Items can jump on or fall off, as you see fit. By writing a new wish list up annually, you give yourself permission to explore new options. Options are good! Treat yourself to a little quality time on your birthday and give some thought to the year ahead of you and what personal and professional successes you might like to see.

★ If you don't start a wish list, you're effectively *limiting* your options at best, and actually *reducing* your options at worst. Think about that for a minute.

So, get those goals and wishes out of your head and onto a list!

Remember that thing you enjoyed when you were a kid, and trust your gut. Don't just let things happen. Look around your life, and be active in the things that you like. Be a finisher! Anyone can start something!

—Frank Pulumbarit, managing principal
www.fpconsultinggroup.com

CHAPTER 5

HOW TO TAKE YOUR WISH LIST TO THE NEXT LEVEL

Now, let's turn that wish list into reality.

KILLER APP ALERT—Crunch Your Goals! Once you have written up your wish list, it's time to do a little **"analysis" on your goals.** Print up your list, get a coloured pen or marker, and start making some notes. For each item you've written down, note three things:

Thing 1: Determine on a scale of one to ten (ten being highest), **how much/how badly** (read: priority) **you want each particular item on your list**. You can have as many tens, nines, eights, etc., as you please. By assigning a "weight" to each item, you will quickly see how high a priority any given item is for you.

Thing 2: Once you have assigned priorities to all your items, go through your list again and **break your list into three columns**: "short-term," "mid-term," and "long-term." Each goal should be placed in the column where you feel it most naturally belongs. Each item on your goals list should be placed in descending order of priority, starting with the tens, then the nines, eights, etc.

Thing 3: Finally, review your list one last time, and **think about what your timelines might be** for the short-, mid-, and longer terms. Write down the timelines that feel most comfortable to you. BTW, only you can determine what the periods of time short-, mid-, and long-term are. It's your wish list! Get down with it.

You will end up with a chart that will look something like this:

Short-Term (Timeline: six months)	Mid-Term (Timeline: 2018-19)	Long-Term (Timeline: (2020+)
Update resume 10/10	Write a blog 10/10	Financial stability 10/10
Start job search 9/10	Develop a personal brand 10/10	Travel 9/10
Bookmark HR website pages 8/10	Take [course] in [x] skill 8/10	Start a business doing [service] for [x audience] 8/10
Build contacts 7/10	Network 7/10	Volunteer in [x] 7/10
Professional Photo 6/10	Flex work hours 6/10	Work/life balance 7/10
Upgrade your marketing tools 6/10	Research [x area of interest] 6/10	[Fitness] 7/10
Etc.	Etc.	Etc.

Now, print it up, and post your "crunched wish list" at eye level just over your computer, so that you see it every day.

" *I live by a credo: no matter what job you take, it should scare the living shit out of you or it's not worth doing. At the end when you're done, you'll realize "hey, I did that. I can do it!" There are attainable goals and learnings to be had.* **"**

—Jeffrey Elliott, chief executive officer
www.tablerockmedia.com

KILLER APP ALERT—Timing! Timing is everything! Mondays through Wednesdays are great job-search/business-development days because everyone is paying attention on the job, and is actively doing business. By Thursday, people are in the thick of it and starting to burn out. Typically on Fridays, people are checked out emotionally. I always do the heavy lifting on my career or business development Monday through Wednesday. Because I'm aware that by Thursday business people are starting to lose steam, I don't try to do business or lead development on that day. I reserve Thursdays for creative development, like blogging, working on product, or marketing my businesses. Friday is more of a "social" day in nature, so I set Fridays aside for networking, when people are happy to take a call, or a coffee or lunch meeting. Or, I take care of administrative tasks on Fridays. You cannot job-search five days a week—you will burn out. You've got to build in some breaks and/or rewards for yourself. Give yourself a day off—you've earned it! But Monday through Wednesday? Burn, baby, burn!

MINDSET ALERT: Regular and consistent scheduling, are the magic (read: discipline) **to accomplishing your goals.** Every week, week over week, it's a great practice to (religiously) devote a half an hour early on Monday mornings to scheduling your activities for the week. Look at your goals list and choose some items from the short- and mid-term items, and, block off specific times in your schedule for specific items—whether it's job search/business development, content creation and/or marketing tools, administering your business, or whatever you feel needs attention on your wish list. Each of these items should get their own dedicated weekly time slot. If you get into the habit of scheduling your goals activities *each week* based on the above rough timing, you will develop this discipline. The more you get used to scheduling your goals into your calendar, the faster they will actually manifest. By doing this every single week, you will see a lot more progress in a year. I dare you to pull this off! You will literally be amazed at what you can accomplish.

Then, take it one step further. Each year on your birthday, take the day to write up and "crunch" your new wish list. Make it a birthday ritual. Invest in yourself. Gift yourself with taking a crack at looking at what your life might look like if you just do.your.homework!

So, time to get friendly with your wish list! Write your goals down, print them up, and assign each item a weight on a scale of one to ten. Put your items into one of three columns: short-term, mid-term, or long-term. Then, assign a timeline to the short-, mid-, and long-term goals.

Congratulations! The heaviest lifting is done!

Crunching your goals is ground zero for career planning.

If you neglect to write up your goals, you won't go anywhere . . . fast!

> *Two thirds of people coast. They reach a certain level of success, think they've made it, and kind of continue on, not exerting any more influence or effort by not moving forward and keeping up to date. Everyone needs to always be moving forward. The moment you stop growing is the moment you begin to slip. And there are always going to be people who are willing to take your place.*

—Alan Cross, broadcaster and music journalist
The Ongoing History of New Music
www.ajournalofmusicalthings.com

Complacency = "settling" IMHO.

CHAPTER 6

WHAT DOES YOUR NAME STAND FOR, REALLY?

What kind of unique, personal contribution do you want to make professionally? What values do you want associated with your professional name?

There is serious merit in spending some time thinking about the "values" you are communicating in the delivery of your particular product or services to your professional community. How do you think others see you? How would you like others to see or describe you? What would you like your work to stand for, over the test of time? Where and how do you truly want to contribute?

From day one with my business, I've held tight to three core values:

1. **Top standard professionalism** in the delivery of my services.

2. **Transparency**: de-mystifying career/job-search best practices.

3. **Inclusion**: everyone is a unique, deserving "someone."

I didn't actually cast these in stone from day one. But these are the themes that have emerged over time, that mean the most to me in terms of my company's "living brand." And I believe these core values, while not explicitly delineated in words, nevertheless implicitly underlie my day-to-day work. My services are customized to the individual needs of my clients. They are tailored to each person's specific job-search challenges, and are designed to offer behind-the-scenes "intel" and best practices to help them effectively manage their careers. My commitment to my industry is (I trust) evidenced, within an inch of my life.

MINDSET ALERT! So—what would you like your professional name to stand for? What values or themes are the most meaningful to you, in the delivery of your craft? Give it some thought. Determining your core values will add some "gravitas" to your overall messaging that others will pick up at the meta-level. It's both a "confidence builder" and a "confidence messenger."

Then there are the times when things go wrong in a job. Some things are beyond your capacity to fix, things for which—right or wrong—you carry the blame. It does happen! So let it happen. Work your way through it. And move on. A couple of years down the road, after you've left the company, it never hurts to call up an old boss or colleague, invite them out to lunch, and address the issue of long ago. Let them know that you regret the situation went down the way it did. Sometimes, you're the only one truly affected by a negative workplace scenario. But sometimes, your boss or former colleague still holds bad feelings years later. I consider it super professional to find a way to make time to address any issues openly, and express your regret for your part in a bad situation. This simple gesture could be the difference between someone always having ill regard for you, and someone who appreciates your honesty and actually changes his or her mind about you, or, opens up to an understanding of the wider context around the negative situation. Pull that Band-Aid off with care and genuine humility. It will add years to your life!

> **"** *I'm sort of old-school, as in . . . hard work will never do you wrong! No matter what field you are in, one tried-and-true winning formula is to establish yourself right away as the one who will do what it takes. You show up first and leave after everyone else. I've always been impressed with the young, hard workers. They are the ones that I give the recommendations, referrals, and job offers to.* **"**
>
> —Alisyn Camerota, CNN anchor
> **www.alisyncamerota.com**
> **www.cnn.com/shows/new-day**

KILLER APP ALERT—Values! In terms of values, I once saw a resume, in which a person had "watermarked" their values in the background of the document. I thought that was a really nice touch, and was impressed with their self-awareness and self-branding capacity.

Take the opportunity to show and tell others that you mean business . . . along with what *kind* of business you mean! Put it in your tag line. Create a living brand . . . as in, *be your brand!*

❝ *Own your mistakes! If you own them, you earn respect. You need to do the right thing, whatever it is that you're doing. Don't take the easy way; take the right way. Be accountable.* **❞**

—Colette Watson, senior vice-president
www.rogersmedia.com

CHAPTER 7

HOW DO YOU "LOOK"?

Now that you've got a your career plan, it's time to develop your brand and sexy-up your marketing mix!

> 66 *Learning about the marketing side of things is just as important as the content side. I wish I'd learned this much earlier.* 99

—Jacky Habib, freelance journalist and entrepreneur
www.newlenstravel.com

In this chapter, we address **developing our personal brand**, i.e., how we appear to others (read: "in person," "on paper," "digitally," and "socially"). We take a hard look at the appearance we project, and then we take our positioning and packaging to the next level by upgrading all of our marketing tools.

Try this exercise: Do a quick and simple Google search for "[current year] resume samples." Then, click on "images." It's great to have a look at what the rest of the workforce is doing with their resumes. Now, compare your existing resume to these samples. You will see that yesterday's "content resumes" have definitely transformed into today's "visual" and/or "info-graphic" resumes. You don't have to like them all. Just browse through and see if there is any one sample—or elements of different samples—that resonate with you. **It's up to you to do a partial or a complete resume makeover,** based on what you like, and how you want to represent yourself. These samples will definitely give you ideas on what you might do to upgrade your resume and brand. That's what we're shooting for: anything from an upgrade, to a full-blown reinvention. Try to strike a balance with the "look" of your marketing tools that feels comfortable to you.

You can buy many of these resume templates on line, if you want to do it yourself. I opted for hiring a graphic designer whose work I had seen and really liked. While I enjoy some aspects of design, the technology side of it isn't really my thing . . .

WHERE TO BEGIN?

If you are going to give your "overall look" a serious review, it's highly recommended that you start from scratch!

Print up all the marketing tools you have, from your resume to your business card, email signature, cover-letter template, website landing page, blog, LinkedIn profile, references, bio—any and all of it. Line them up beside each other on your desk and take a good long look at how comprehensive they are in terms of up-to-date content. Take another long look at how consistently formatted and branded they are.

Building a brand is not terribly complicated, although when you first do it, it can be a little daunting. You need to decide on a typeface, font size, and signature colour (or colours) to give your marketing tools some "pop." You can incorporate visuals like "icons" to represent social media platforms. Your marketing tools should be consistently laid out and formatted, with appropriate white space. Your full contact info (no physical addresses, please!) and web presence should be front and centre.

A little humour: I swear that when I die, my last words are going to be "put your @#$% contact information on your @#$% correspondence!" In other words, please set your friends and colleagues up for success by being a professional, and ensuring that no one ever has to go digging for your contact info. And, yes, that even applies to your personal email. Why lose the opportunity to brand yourself any chance you can get? Adopt a nice, professional "signature" with full contact info. (Insert recruiter sigh of relief.)

Once you decide on a "look," you can easily apply/adapt that look to all your other marketing tools. The trick is to be consistent. View these marketing tools as vehicles that will help increase your visibility and build positive engagement with potential employers and business contacts.

KILLER APP ALERT—Visuals: More and more, people are incorporating visuals into their marketing tools (read: hotlinks, graphic elements, word clouds, logos, icons, tag lines, titles, banners, newsletter, blog and/or podcast hotlinks, memes, photos, videos). Be this person! Shake it up. *Check with your gut . . . do you like the way your marketing tools look and feel?* If so, go with them. I'm always pleasantly surprised when someone injects a creative touch into his or her marketing pieces. I don't mean "over-the-top" visuals—just a personal stamp and/or "visual relief".

★ **Don't let anyone scare you about the use of photos.** If you've got a *professional* headshot that you feel accurately represents you, use it. If you don't want to include a photo, don't. It's your resume. What is your gut telling you? Some people are afraid that if they add a photo, it will lend bias to their candidacy. Perhaps it will. But if there is bias afoot, best to let it happen at the resume-submission stage, instead of after you have gotten your hopes up and have been called to interview. Always get ahead of the process—you know?

Establishing your look and managing your brand will be well received by the professionals reviewing them. The amount of work you put into your brand will show. It will tell others that you're a diligent, thoughtful professional who understands the need to build, showcase, and leverage (read: maximize) a brand. It will also communicate that you understand the value of branding in general, and as a result, will probably impress a hiring manager with your inherent understanding of brand management.

"MARKETING TOOLS" NEEDED WHEN SEEKING STAFF JOBS:

You will need a **resume** (PDF format), references, a long-format **bio**; **cover email**/cover letter (the best suggestion is to put your cover letter and resume in *one* PDF file and send by email), a **business card**, a professional **voice-mail** message, an **email signature** with full contact information, **hotlinks** to web pages that showcase samples of work you have created and/or delivered, and a **LinkedIn profile.**

★ **Never underestimate the value of LinkedIn endorsements and recommendations.** When I recruit, I definitely take a look at who is endorsing your skills (read: how many individuals are actually lending you "social proof"). I also definitely review recommendations from your colleagues and peers, to see what they have to say about you.

"MARKETING TOOLS" NEEDED TO MARKET YOUR PRODUCT/ SERVICES AS AN ENTREPRENEUR/FREELANCER:

You will need "**written copy**" that outlines your product and/ or service (read: some all-purpose narrative that you can use in all your marketing tools to describe your product/services); **testimonials** (one-liners from *top* brands, names, reputations, and titles—go for the gold, always!); a **bio** (in short, medium, and long formats), a "**business-development email template**" which introduces/outlines your product/service to prospective clients; a **business card**; an **internet presence** on Facebook, YouTube, Instagram, and/or Twitter, etc.; an **email signature** with full contact information; a **voice-mail** message; and, finally, a **web page**, site, or blog. If you are going all in with your business, you will probably want to develop some **"swag"** (promotional items) too, like banners for conferences, branded pens, branded memory sticks, etc. You get the idea.

Below is a handy list of all the "self-marketing tools" you will need for a job search for full-time/staff roles, juxtaposed with the marketing tools that you will need for business development, in order to build and market your own small business as a freelancer, contractor, or as an entrepreneur.

How many of these marketing tools you create, and how many platforms you choose to be on, is up to you. IMHO the more the better. You don't have to create all your marketing tools at once, but do get at it by including them in your short- to mid-term goals list. Give yourself a year to get them all up and running properly. Develop a look for all your marketing tools, and stick to it like glue. Then review all your marketing tools annually, for content and consistency.

STAFF MARKETING TOOLS V. FREELANCE MARKETING TOOLS

CV/Resume (PDF format)

Develop some **"copy"** that outlines your product, service, or both.

Verbal references and/or written recommendations. Note: Verbal recs now trump [sic] written recs!

Client testimonials—written "one-liners" from *top* brands, names, reputations, and/or titles

Bio (long format)

Bio (long, medium, and short formats)

Cover Email ("cover email" replaces the old-school "cover letter," unless a separate Word. doc is specifically requested). Just put your cover letter copy into a fresh email and attach your resume in .PDF format.

Business Introduction email—I'm writing to introduce you to [your company name]. Our company's primary services include [list services and/or product]. Add a call to action/incentive and your contact info and you're done!

LinkedIn Profile: complete, and up to date. Note: You should have as many endorsements and written recommendations from peers and/or direct reports as possible.

Social Media: A freelancer is likely to have Facebook and Twitter profiles, and possibly Instagram, too, depending on the market that applies to your specific product and/or service.

Internet Presence: Create hotlinks to electronic samples of your work. By 2020, you will probably need video, too. Just sayin'.

Internet Presence: Web page/ Website/Blog/YouTube channel/ Pinterest/Google My Business (as applicable)

Email "signature," including any brand elements/visuals, and *full* contact information. Do not miss an opportunity to brand your full name on your emails.

Email "signature," including any brand elements/visuals, and *full* contact information. Do not miss an opportunity to brand your full name on your emails.

Business Card—always!

Business Card—always!

Professional Headshot	Professional Headshot
	Photographic a/o graphic images (high-res JPG or GIF formats) to promote your product and/ or services
Voice-mail message	**Voice-mail** message
	Promotional items/swag

Internet Presence: Give some serious thought to participating as actively as possible on social media. Publishing a blog and/ or taking the opportunity to write editorials are great ways to build your name and "street creds." Get yourself out there! Then, add hotlinks to these items in your e-signature.

Please remember that your name is your brand. Use your first and last name at every opportunity when answering calls, include your full name in your email signature block, and always state your full name and company name when introducing yourself verbally and/or in writing. Seriously, please be this person!

MINDSET ALERT: Your signature "look" evolves over time, just like you do. Get the first iteration of your brand completed on all your marketing pieces (read: yay, re-invention!), and then be sure to review all your marketing tools annually on your birthday. Scrubbing your marketing tools annually will ensure your brand evolves along with you, and that it stays organic and current, and incorporates best practices year over year. If you are dissatisfied with any particular aspect of your brand, you are always welcome to "morph it" as you see fit. Once a year and you're done—much preferable to the constant dribble of little bits and pieces, hither and thither, all of the time. Just get your marketing tools done, and you're good to go for the next twelve months!

Every time you upgrade or add to your brand, it gives you the opportunity to promote it (anew) to your professional circle. Think about that . . . I morph my brand every few years to keep my market on its toes.

> " *Entrepreneurial training is key. Even as a working professional, I'm constantly taking online courses that help me sharpen my skills and learn about business and marketing. I also work with coaches who are experts in these areas, and these investments have made a huge difference in my career.*"
>
> —Jacky Habib, freelance journalist and entrepreneur
> **www.newlenstravel.com**

Now, let's think about Jacky's comment for a minute: Why wouldn't you hire someone to help you? What is it exactly, that is stopping you from getting the help and/or training that you need?

CHAPTER 8

YOUR RESUME: GROUND ZERO FOR REINVENTION!

Here's how to set yourself up for success with all your marketing tools.

ALWAYS START WITH YOUR RESUME "CONTENT"

Resumes are still necessary and will remain so for the foreseeable future. Even when we reach the point where physical resumes are no longer being used, you will still need to create "resume content" for social media profiles, etc., that outlines your experience. So having a baseline (resume) Word document is a great way to kick-start, gather together, and maintain the content that best represents your professional experience.

Print up the content from your previous resume to use as a reference point, but start a fresh template—i.e., ★ don't use an old template with a bunch of "legacy formatting" buried in the Word document (from all the changes you've made to it over time) that can jam up applicant-tracking systems. In other words: get ahead of the process!

Open with your name and contact information. Make sure your name stands out above all by using a larger type font and possibly a colour. **Add your title** if you can, to give the reader a sense of the skills and knowledge you have. Leave your physical address behind. **Add full contact information—** don't just give your mobile number and email address. Skype? Facebook? Twitter? LinkedIn profile? If you've got them, list them. Business colleagues will use any and all methods to contact you. Be accessible!

★ Please don't add a telephone "landline" unless you are there during business hours to answer it.

★ Many job seekers use the same old "content resume" they've developed through the years, adding to and/or deleting items as they go along. Many set up a LinkedIn profile and then neglect to update it over time. Most job seekers are not even aware of the many tools they have at their disposal to market their skills and, further, have not yet learned how to market themselves on all the digital platforms that are now available. Most don't do annual "scrubs" on all their marketing tools. Their loss!

MINDSET ALERT—Job Titles: Lots of people have told me that while they were performing a certain role for a company, the role itself was much, much more than the title reflected. This is very common—employers have been cross-pollenating jobs for years! Example: I once had the title "operations manager," but was actually fulfilling a general manager's role. So on my resume I combine the two, and list it as "operations/general manager." And I can defend that quite comfortably in any interview. I'm happy to explain the mash-up . . . because *I am the one who is always in charge of my message, and I'm not shy to deliver it.*

Further, I don't see a lot of people listing their "title" on their resumes and email signatures. Why is that? Cultural artifact? I strongly recommend you use your title wherever you can. It helps other people understand what you do, right out of the gate, instead of leaving readers to do the math.

MINDSET ALERT—Career Trajectories: Many people express anxiety over their job history/histories. They often feel that their history is "disparate" or "disjointed" in that their career doesn't follow a particular, accepted path. Example: They tried "this", ended up in "that", then redirected their efforts in yet another area ... and they feel that the "thread" of their experience doesn't make sense. This is very common. Careers, especially in the early years, are all about experimentation. Don't worry about the "appearance" of your career moves. *Context is what's important.* How did I move from television production, to business operations, to recruiting? As far as I'm concerned, it was a natural progression over 20 years ... easily "defensible" through the course of my career. I loved the product of "television production". But I found that I hated the production process. So I eventually moved into the business side of television, which fit more naturally with my interests. One of the business aspects of television that impacted me the most was "talent acquisition." So, 15 years later, I ended up as a recruiter and career coach. Makes sense to me! It will to others too, who take the time to digest the "context" of your career. In time, you will become more adept at representing that context, and your career moves, as well. Bottom line: All experience is valuable, defensible, and adds to the aggregate of your experience. Any and all experience is invaluable. And don't let others scare you with their expectations. Seriously. It's your story, not theirs.

KILLER APP ALERT—Write up Your Profile! It's time to draft your story . . . and we have an app for that! Back in the day, people would start their resume with an "Objective." Today, that has been replaced with a "Summary Profile."

Your profile should tell your story in three short sentences:

1. Who you are (now, at this point in time/what you currently do);

2. What you've done (in the past); and

3. What you want (in the future) (aka positioning yourself for next career move—lateral or up!)

MINDSET ALERT—Copy Writing: If you're going to participate in business, please get used to "drafting copy," even if it's about yourself. Every businessperson needs to get comfortable with drafting content. And the only way to do that is to flex the muscle with practice. (If you've written up your goals, you already have "draft copy" for #3 above—i.e., "what you want").

Just write it up. Throw down whatever ideas you have onto a page, and expect the first draft to be . . . not very good (remember, an empty page is worse). Over time, you can enhance your profile by tightening it up with descriptors, quantifiers, and/or qualifiers.

Your profile is the best all-purpose marketing tool you can have. Your profile is as organic as you are, and should evolve along with you: just get the first iteration drafted. It will definitely be the hardest copy you will ever have to write. Everyone struggles with writing a profile statement (especially Canadians—we are far too humble). Work.that.muscle.

Once your story is complete, you can migrate it from your resume to the "Profile/Summary" section of your LinkedIn account and/or onto a web page. You can also use it as your elevator pitch and/or use it when networking.

> " *Prior to being introduced to the concept of 'writing a profile' on my resume, I had just listed a whole bunch of functional skillsets. [Then] I identified five or six highlights and crafted them into an executive summary/ profile statement at the top of my resume. I use that statement as a pitch whenever I am out networking. It's kind of a "highlight reel" or "trailer" that I have about things I've accomplished, which helps me properly represent my key strengths and successes.* "

—Towa Beer, president
www.mymentorsaid.ca

HARD SKILLS & SOFT SKILLS

For the next section of your resume content, list your hard and soft skills.

KILLER APP ALERT—How to Figure Out Your Hard Skills: Some people find it difficult to figure out their skills. If this is the case for you, simply **go back in your mind to each of the jobs you've ever done, and write down what you knew you were really good at in that job.** Say, in one job you were known for your customer service. "Customer service" is better known today as "customer relationship management (CRM)." So jot that down. In another job, you were really good at streamlining in-house processes. So, "operations management" or "trouble-shooting" is one of your skills. Maybe in one job you were good at team building—aka leadership! In another role, you managed a situation in which your company's brand was affected—this can be called "reputation management" or "crisis management." Another example would be if you were really good at report writing, or managing documentation/ records. These become "report drafting" or "electronic records management." All you have to do is go back through all your gigs and **write down what you know you were really good at—and then find a current business term to describe it.** If you're struggling with finding these terms, check out online university business programs. Their courses offer current terms that will help you craft a more accurate and up-to-date representation of your skills and knowledge.

Or . . . **go through job descriptions** for roles similar to your own. The wording is all there. All you have to do is tailor the particular skill to your experience, and give it a more appropriate, formal, or up-to-date name. Sexy those skills up already!

Soft skills, on the other hand, are personal characteristics and/ or personality traits that you use day to day, that make it possible for you to work well with others—something employers are always looking for. Soft skills include things like accountability, time management, initiative, motivation, drive, flexibility, resilience, coping skills, and effective communication.

Other positive attributes or **"life skills"** include stress management, healthy self-esteem, self-awareness, etiquette, good manners, adaptability, collaboration, a "can-do" attitude, wellness best practices, and (the all-critical, in-demand) empathy.

Corporate soft skills include strategic awareness, information management, political sensitivity, discretion, conflict resolution, the ability to help others "save face," the ability to actively listen, sensitivity to market timing, language skills, cultural knowledge and social graces, and staying on corporate brand. **Corporate hard skills** include things like public relations/crisis management, public speaking and debating, problem solving, critical thinking and decision-making. Developing additional skills will stand you in very good stead, if you are shooting for upper management.

> *I've seen professionals lose their jobs because they couldn't handle criticism—they were too sensitive to it. Sooner or later, someone above you is going to come and tear your vision to shreds, and you need to be able to handle that. Persistence is key! You really need a mixture of persistence to get it done, but you also need sensitivity to the people around you."*

—Paula Virany, video producer/editor/director

> *It's a long journey. You have to get along with people. You have to work with people. I've seen a couple of colleagues effectively destroy their careers by losing it and not keeping their emotions in check. I've seen it happen. Losing your temper over ultimately stupid things. You'll get the heave-ho."*

—David Onley, senior lecturer
www.utoronto.ca

In other words, get it (and keep it) together.

Strong soft skills are one of the most determining factors when it comes to a successful hire. The more you have, the better. Know what your soft skills are, and be prepared/find a way to communicate them to hiring managers.

Putting some time into taking a fresh look at your hard and soft skills is a worthy exercise. First, it pushes you to take your game to a new level. Second, it gives you permission to reinvent yourself. Remember, we all grow and change. Allow yourself the opportunity to recognize that "that was then" and "this is now" when it comes to representing your knowledge and skills. Feel free to up your game! Your self-esteem will thank you. Give yourself some credit, already.

Reality Check: Ponder this for a moment: I bet my last buck that the person (you are) who got out of bed *yesterday* morning is not the same person (you are) who got out of bed *this* morning. Right? It's good to grow and change. If you didn't, I'd actually have reason to be worried about you.

Please know that you can have anywhere from "some exposure" to "deep experience" in any given skill. Here's an example: As a recruiter in the Canadian cultural sector, I often have to ask candidates if they speak French. Candidates will frequently reply: "I don't really have French." "Now, what does that mean exactly?" I'll ask. They'll answer: "Well, I have some French—I understand *un petit peu*, but I can't write in French." Fair enough. **But don't minimize or negate any capacity to communicate in a different language!** You don't have to be perfect. I once got a senior level job on the strength of the fact that I was able to speak conversational French. Could I write regulatory copy or draft policy in French?

Mon Dieu, non! But I did have rusty, conversational French and it turned out that it was a serious value-add in a job that interfaced with the Canadian government on a regular basis. French Canadian stakeholders all thought my accent was "charming". However imperfect my delivery, my attempts to converse in their language impressed them. It enabled them to "relate" to me and, as a result, they accepted me into their fold. I was one of their tribe! Yay! To this day, I'm happy to dive into speaking "Franglais" — aka "moitié-moitié." I know my French is imperfect. But I go there just the same. And Francophones truly appreciate it. (Shout out to my parents and the first Trudeau government for ensuring I had exposure to the French language as a child. They did me an incredible, life-long service.) If such is the case for you, for heaven's sakes, don't minimize your abilities—or any other skill.

> **"** *It's the four Cs that are really critical in professional development: communications, creativity, critical thinking, and cultural fluency. We really are in a different era, in which we are building careers for life. We're seeing the biggest change since the industrial revolution. As professionals, it's about becoming agile and adapting. It's going to be rare that any professional remains static for even a five-year period.* **"**

—Caroline Konrad, director, Career & Co-op Centre
www.ryerson.ca

HARDWARE, SOFTWARE, TECHNOLOGY SKILLS & TECHNOLOGY PLATFORMS

This is the section of your resume in which you list the **hardware and software programs** you're capable of using, as well as any **technology platforms** that you are able to work on. Employers and recruiters *want and need to know* the tech skills and platforms that you can use, as unique sectors tend to use unique technologies.

So, make it easy on recruiters and hiring managers and set readers up for success by listing your tech skills and platforms. Do you use Google Docs? Outlook? GoToMeeting? Conference calls? Photoshop? Electronic calendars? Salesforce? QuickBooks? Facebook Live? Snapchat? Pinterest? E-commerce platforms like PayPal or other forms of electronic banking? WhatsApp? Tumblr? Instagram? Twitter Periscope? Skype? 4Square? Any and all and more of these are incredibly important—**don't undersell, neglect or bury your own capacity.**

The more adept and knowledgeable you become, and the more you have to offer, the better your standing in the workforce of the future. Allow yourself to grow.

> *Technology is increasingly important, as is the ability to adapt to and use technology. Another area is interpersonal skills: the ability to interact with people, and to adapt to different situations. A second language will be increasingly important, too. If you were to think about where the shift of commercial influence is going to be around the world,*

English may remain dominant, but Chinese and Spanish are likely to be as influential."

—Andy Robling, vice-president, client development
www.hays.com

WORK HISTORY (AKA "PROFESSIONAL EXPERIENCE")

Now it's time to **list your professional experience in reverse chronological order.** Stick to three or four bullet points *only* for each job, and make sure those bullet points don't just reflect your "responsibilities", but also reflect any "accomplishments" you had within those roles. Add dates on the right margin (it's not necessary to indicate months), and add visuals like logos or hotlinks to companies, where possible.

★ **Get rid of any old jobs** that are no longer applicable to the field you're pursuing (especially student jobs, unless they relate directly to your current career trajectory).

★ **Don't make the copy so dense that it's hard to read.** "White space" is known to be user-friendly; it helps keep the document from looking crammed. Scrub your copy, and take out every extraneous detail or word you can—help the document breathe!

Recruiters and hiring managers spend an approximate eight seconds reading your resume. Make it easy for them to read the document, and to find the details in your work experience that they are looking for. They don't want every.single.detail. They want clear, obvious skills and coherent, informative copy. Set them (as well as yourself) up for success.

EDUCATION & PROFESSIONAL DEVELOPMENT

Next up in your resume content is the **Education & Professional Development section**—these two go hand in hand. As a recruiter, I'm obviously interested in your educational background. But if I were to have to choose between two candidates—one with the (appropriate) education, and one with the same educational creds as well as a good array of professional development—the choice would be clear. Door #2 it is!

List all of your education, as well as any certificates, courses, seminars, webinars, conferences, and/or awards that you've attended or achieved—no matter how big or small. Employers want to know that you are a "life-long learner." It will also "signal" an employer that one of your requirements in future jobs (mid-term goals) is ongoing professional development, which you can negotiate into your deal. ★ That being said, it's best not to rely on any employer to provide training. Take charge of ongoing training yourself.

Acquiring business knowledge has a powerful impact on your self-esteem. It increases your confidence and your marketability. It adds to overall job security. It "rounds you out" professionally and definitely takes your game to the next level. Business knowledge and business acumen are mission-critical to building the bench strength needed to sustain your career. Be proactive and **set clear-cut goals each year for professional development**. Choose opportunities that build your education, experience, and exposure, either formally (accredited) or informally ("street-creds"), or both. Repeat! Obtaining informal street creds is a great way to help transition your existing skills from one sector/industry to another (read: transferrable *skills* + transferrable *knowledge*).

> " Try to be aware of the full extent and scope of the industry you're in. I tried to learn as much about every possible aspect of the industry and parts of the business as I could. There's absolutely no reason today not to know. Start digging around. One thing leads to another; information is key to success!"

—David Kines, president and co-founder
www.hollywoodsuite.ca

Stop for a minute, and please re-read David's quote. He has built an incredibly successful career on the strength of acquiring knowledge, combined with taking risks. So smart!

Formal accreditation can be obtained through certificate and degree/post-grad courses, fellowships, seminars/webinars, and workshops—all of which are more accessible than ever. **Shop wisely for programs, and if need be, start a crowdfunding campaign to finance it.** ★ Never, ever shy away from investing in yourself.

Informal accreditation comes from participation on industry boards, committees, panels, and public service/volunteer efforts. You may also find opportunities to participate in initiatives in your current workplace. Think about any internal challenges your company is currently experiencing. Is there a problem you have a solution to? Are there any special projects or an internal task force you can participate in?

Serious professionals are taking increasing ownership of their careers by proactively driving their professional development. Make a concerted effort to stay on top of your industry's developments. Look into areas where the professional and trade associations are putting their focus. Stay up to date by reading industry-specific articles and downloading current industry reports, forecasts, and white papers. Believe me, it will put you at the front of the employment line!

The best possible strategy to commit to, bar none, is life-long learning. Acquiring business knowledge and broadening your education are the single most important things you can do to increase your earnings through the course of your career.

> 66 *Join a trade association and become an industry advocate. Be an active participant in the industry by becoming engaged in the community, with an aim to better understand the subtleties of legacy issues, current trends, and future business models.* 99
>
> —Christa Dickenson, executive director
> **www.telefilm.ca**

Exactement, Madame!

PUBLIC SERVICE (AKA "VOLUNTEER ROLES") & PROFESSIONAL MEMBERSHIPS

Finally, you can add a section to your resume content that outlines any **public service** you've done **and/or professional memberships** you hold. Sometimes, people are reticent to add volunteer work to their resume because they think it may be perceived as inferior, or they just don't want to bring attention to unpaid work. Fair enough. But anyone who has volunteered anywhere, knows that it can be anywhere from pretty demanding to all-encompassing work. So take pride in it, add it to your resume, and call it public service—because that's what it is (paid or unpaid). As well, list any associations, guilds, unions, boards, or committees you've participated in. Employers view these types of professional experiences as serious "value-adds."

VISUALS

OK, almost done. The last overall "scrub" or "edit" to your resume content is to **add visuals.** These could include: formatting/layout, icons, logos, graphic layout, colours, fonts, and hyperlinks to work samples, where possible. Incorporate whatever graphic/marketing elements you can that will provide the reader with "visual relief." Visuals make the overall read more interesting and compelling. So, mix in some visuals with your content.

★ **Do not neglect to run spelling and grammar checks on your resume, ever!** It is commonly known that when a recruiter or hiring manager sees a typo or grammar issue on someone's correspondence, it is a clear sign that they are "half-milers"— i.e., they don't do a thorough, complete job. If the resume/cover in front of me is really stellar, I might forgive a slip up. But, truly, it leaves a distinctly negative impression. As they say in television, "600 sets of eyes in the edit suite are never enough!" Ask someone else (preferably a senior colleague) to proofread your resume content. That one mistake can turn a "yes-interview" candidate into a "maybe-interview" candidate—or, it can take you right out of the running.

★ **In saving your document, don't name the file "resume."** If you do, recruiters will never be able to find it by searching your name in their computer. Remember: your name is your brand, right? Wield it! **Save the file in PDF format using your full name:** "Smith, Jane resume CBC-cover.pdf," and you're done (unless, of course, they specifically ask for a Word document).

You've now got the first iteration of your reinvented resume, complete with a "look" and/or "brand."

Félicitations!

CHAPTER 9

MIGRATING YOUR BRAND TO ALL YOUR MARKETING TOOLS

Once you've established a new look for your resume, it's easy to migrate that "look" to all your other marketing tools.

That same "look" from the top of your resume can easily be re-purposed as a template—or "letterhead," if you will—for your cover letter. It can also be the "header" on your list of references, as well as your bio—using the exact same layout, with your name, title, and all your contact information. Migrate that same "look" or elements of that look even further—to your email signature, your business card, and your web page or blog.

All of your marketing tools need to reflect the same "signature look"—that's what constitutes/establishes your brand.

I cannot stress the importance of using "visuals" enough. Try to build a small library of visuals that you can use to enhance your documents, e-transmissions, etc. These can include word clouds, logos, graphic layout, icons, hotlinks to newsletters, your blog, videos and/or podcasts, memes, wordclouds or "wordles", a tag line, JPG or GIF photo/images, a LinkedIn profile hotlink—whatever visuals work for you, that you can use to enhance your brand. All your marketing pieces should be similar in look, consistent in their layout, with full contact info and web presence front and centre.

Your "signature look" will evolve over time, just as you will. So it's a simple case of "scrubbing" your marketing pieces once a year (I reserve the time around my birthday to do this, along with renewing my goals list). Completing this annual scrub of your marketing tools will ensure that your brand evolves with you over time, that your brand stays current with market best practices year over year, and actually supports you in delivering on your career objectives!

> *Up until I got some help with my career, I was just going from job to job. I worked hard, but I'd never actually thought of a strategy before . . . As in, here's the way to lay out your resume effectively, here's a strategy to build your brand—looking at it all from a very strategic approach. Everything from resume writing and building my website, to managing my brand—I definitely apply all these tools today!*

—Kevin O'Keefe, producer/director
www.kevinokeefe.tv

HOW TO WRITE A COVER LETTER

What is the point of writing a cover letter anymore? Many people wonder if they even get read. They also wonder why they can't just send a resume and be done with it. Well, the short answer is yes, you can just send a resume. *But why miss out on the chance to show a hiring committee that not only do your skills match the job description (making you shortlistable), but also that your career aspirations and intentions are a match with their company?* That, friends, is the sweet spot! Employers are looking for cultural fit and alignment with their business goals. And we can see from your skills that you *can* do the job, but what we really need to know is: *will* you do the job? Your cover letter/cover email is a great way to show and tell employers that your career intentions and aspirations fit with the company. And why. And how. This will show that you've done your homework, and they will recognize and appreciate it.

Some recruiters read cover letters, and some don't. It's not a one-size-fits-all kind of situation. As *a* recruiter, I read your cover letters because I want as much information on you as possible. As *your* recruiter, I'm working hard to ensure that once you take the job on, you will stay in it—and give my client a return on their investment in you. And I don't mean stay three months. It takes time to master any given role. My expectation is that you are going to stay with that company two to five years. And you won't stay if you haven't done your homework on your goals and the company, and haven't determined that this is the *exact opportunity* you want and need to take your career to the next level. Which is, by the way, the desired win-win for everyone concerned—not to mention *your responsibility*. With a longer-term commitment, the job seeker gets to develop deeper subject matter expertise on the job, further their individual professional goals, and the employer doesn't have to deal with costly personnel changes and the inherent administrative burden. So, yes, I'm checking out all your stuff: Your cover letter, your LinkedIn profile, your recommendations *and* endorsements, your resume, your interests, what groups you participate in. All.of.it.

★ **Never delay applying,** or submit an application on the last available date (deadline) on the posting. Hiring these days is pretty rapid fire. Getting last-minute applications is a pain in the butt for most recruiters. You heard it here first.

KILLER APP ALERT—How to Write a Cover Letter! Follow the outline below, and just get it done. Throw down your first draft. You can expect the first version to be not.so.great. That's totally normal, and expected. Here's an easy five-point check list:

1. Salutation + Introduction

2. Qualifications

3. Value Adds

4. Close with your "Business Case"

5. Sign off

Keep it to one page (a page and half for more senior roles, max).

Open your cover letter with a greeting/salutation, and make it "warm and social" in nature—i.e., not overly stiff or formal. Then, a line or two to introduce yourself and *provide some context* as to why you are writing to them: "I'm applying to [job posting], posted in [x]." Or, you can mention who referred the job posting to you, as in: "I am applying for [role], and I'm indebted to [x] for their referral" (a little formal, but you get the idea). You can also go the less formal route, and simply convey your interest/excitement in a particular role, with this particular company. However you open your cover letter, be sure to offer context! As a recruiter, I appreciate knowing *why* or *how* you to came to write me.

The next paragraph should address the match between your (strongest) skills and the actual requirements of the job (refer to Chapter 15's: "Can You Make the Shortlist?"*).*

You can use the second paragraph to showcase your "value-adds": Attributes, skills, and knowledge that maybe aren't even required, but the company would benefit from knowing anyway, like additional languages you can speak, or what your management style is like. Offer some qualifiers on what kind of mindset you would bring to the job. This is the paragraph in which you let them know what kind of person you are, what values you have, what your work ethic is like. Keep it short, pointed and honest.

KILLER APP WITHIN A KILLER APP ALERT—How to Make Your Business Case (Within Your Cover Letter)! The last paragraph of a cover letter is used to tie it all together and deliver your business case: Why you (what's unique about your candidacy)? Why now (how does this opportunity fit into your career path)? Why this role in particular? Why this company in particular? Google their website. Check their "About Us" page and read their mission statement. If it resonates with you, tie that into why you want to work with the company, in writing, in your closing paragraph.

Most people don't formulate a business case for themselves. By including your business case in the last paragraph of your cover letter, you are making it easier on hiring managers *by telling them why they should hire you*, rather than leaving it to them to figure out whether or not to hire you. Think about that. Take the power into your own hands and offer up some good reasons for them to give you serious consideration. If you neglect to write up your business case, you are leaving it to the employer to decide why they should like you over someone else. You won't have any say, because you didn't do your homework and haven't told them so—and it shows! So tell them why you're a better hire than anyone else. Make your business case. IMHO, making your business case is more important than anything. It's career activism at its finest.

Once your draft cover/email letter is complete, you need to do a serious "content edit": Go through the cover letter and scrub out every single extraneous word that you can. This will lighten the copy up, create white space/balance, and reduce the amount of work the person has to do in reading your letter. Think concise! Think brevity! Remember, you only have eight seconds to get and keep their attention.

When your content edit is done, go back through one final time and **scrub your salutation and sign-off,** and be sure to make them "social in nature." Salutations/introductions and sign-offs are warmer and less formal these days. Take the opportunity to connect in a meaningful way with the hiring manager. Authenticity always rules. So out with the old "To whom it may concern" and in with something personalized that is warm, friendly, generous, engaging, or *compelling* in some way. Find a way to get their (favourable) attention! If it's the job of your dreams, talk to them straight from your heart.

Run a spelling and grammar check—always.

If you have branded letterhead, use it. If you don't, think about creating a cover letter template for yourself that matches your overall brand/resume (formatting, fonts, graphics, icons . . . and visuals).

Save your cover letter *and* resume in *one* file, in PDF format, and call the file "[last name], [first name] Cover [Company name].PDF." You'll look organized and professional. And, most importantly, by naming the file with your first and last name, you will be searchable by name in your recruiter's computer. For heavens' sakes, don't call the file "[initials] resume." Enough said.

HOW TO WRITE A BIO (YOUR BIOGRAPHY)

Bios are amazing marketing tools! If you don't have one, I urge you to indulge. You will be amazed at how you feel about yourself when you see the final product.

A bio can really help you see yourself in a new light—it is fantastic for your professional self-esteem. Your bio is your story. Almost anything goes, but if you stick to the below broad categories, you'll be covered. If you are missing information for any one of the sections, don't worry about it, just skip it, move onto the next section and don't sweat it . . .

A bio should always be written *in the third person*. When possible, it should also be written *by a third person*—i.e., not you! Ideally, you will get a communications professional to write a bio for you, as a paid service. This is one document that you want to invest in outsourcing to a professional writer/public relations person, if you can afford it. At worst, we all misrepresent ourselves, and at best, we short-change ourselves when drafting up our marketing tools. This is no time to be humble.

You can choose to write your bio yourself if you like, using the below format, but a professional communications person will see things in you and your portfolio that you just can't. Or don't. Or won't. Most job seekers are handicapped by low self-esteem. So invest in yourself, and get some qualitative help. You'll be very glad you did.

The following is a handy guide-track for writing the different sections a bio:

Bio Section 1 - List **your name and current title, position, or role**, and develop a short piece of narrative about the services or product that you offer (refer to Chapter 8's "Resume Content—How to Write up Your Profile Statement"). Highlight and showcase any special expertise, experience, knowledge, or skills you have that set you apart from others in your peer group and/or functional area.

Bio Section 2 - Use this section to write up your **work history—** from most recent to oldest—in prose format. Start with what you are doing now, then go back through your work history (the ones you want to list) in reverse chronological order, and provide a short description of each role role, the company, your length of time in it, and successes and/or accomplishments within those roles.

Bio Section 3 - Professional "Chops": In this section, and as applicable, describe your participation on any boards, committees, memberships, professional associations, volunteer and/or community work, guilds, unions, working groups, task forces, etc. You could also mention any awards, commendations, or honours that you have earned.

Bio Section 4 - Outline your languages and education (read: degrees, diplomas, certificates), including any academic distinctions, as well as any applicable **professional development**

or specialized training you have taken, that you feel is important to highlight.

Bio Section 5 - End your bio with a short "**personal piece**" that offers some context as to your physical location and/or interests. Add something here that tells them who you are as a person. Example: "Michelle lives north of Toronto with her beautiful German shepherd, Stella, and spends all her spare time working in animal rescue and animal advocacy." If you can tie the narrative into a personal "greater purpose," that's even better. Mentioning your geographical location also offers valuable context.

Bio Section 6 - Add your **full contact information.** Knowing your story isn't going to help you advance if they don't know how or where to find you.

Professional Photo: Be sure to **add a good-quality/high-res photo** if you have one. It can be placed at the top or bottom of your bio. A photo helps others identify you when you show up to speak at, or moderate, an industry panel. Some will argue that a photo lends bias, and they wouldn't necessarily be wrong. Bias doesn't happen much, but it does happen—it can exist just about anywhere. But think of it this way: if a decision-maker is going to lend bias by "judging" your photograph, better it happens at the initial stages of any process than the later stages . . . like, after you've gotten your hopes up. If you do come from a minority group, this can be seen as a tremendous "value add" by organizations that encourage and practice true diversity in the workplace. Take heart: more often than not, people do the right thing . . .

Run those spelling and grammar checks. Remember: "Six hundred sets of eyes in the edit suite are never enough."

Once your (long-format) bio is written to your satisfaction, consider revising it into short and medium versions, too. Shortened versions will come in handy if you are invited to participate in conferences/panels or the like. They will want you to submit a bio, and will usually give you a sense of how many words they can accommodate in their marketing pieces. I always have a short (approximately 200 words), medium (approximately 500 words), and long (approximately 800 words) version of my bio, so that I don't have to recreate the wheel every time I'm asked for it. Be sure to give your bio an annual "scrub" to check that all contact information is up to date, and that it fits into the overall "look" of all your other marketing tools.

A professional bio is an often-overlooked marketing tool. You can use your bio for a range of purposes. You can add it to your job-search marketing pieces, and/or enclose it with your CV in a job application. You can add it as a page on your website, and add a hotlink to it in your email signature. You can attach your bio to proposals, articles or blogs you have written. Others can use the document to summarize your expertise when they introduce you at public-speaking events. Just having a bio can make a serious difference in how others perceive you. In my opinion, if you have a professionally written bio, you've arrived (and you're also well ahead of the pack.)

In short, a professionally written bio gives you "gravitas."

HOW TO WRITE A PROFESSIONAL RECOMMENDATION

Here's a handy little four-part format for writing a professional recommendation—whether you are writing it for a peer or colleague, or if someone you have asked for a recommendation asks you to draft it on their behalf. (This happens a lot!)

1. Introduction

2. Body of recommendation: key points and context to message

3. Working rapport/statement of relationship

4. Wrap-up and sign-off

Intro: I am [pleased—or qualifier of choice] to provide the following recommendation for [name].

Body: [name] and I had the pleasure of working together for [length of time] at [company name or project where you met]. Then, offer some context by adding a description of your **working relationship**—i.e., were you peers/colleagues, or was this person your boss, or someone who directly reported to you? Context always wins the day. It warms a person up to you, and makes you less of a stranger.

Next, include a **statement about the kind of working rapport** the two of you had on the job. Mention any qualifiers and/or skills that stood out in your view. And add any favourable personality traits this person has and/or mention your thoughts on their working style, like their reliability, or professionalism, or . . .

Closure/Sign-Off: Make a statement about how you might feel if you had the opportunity to work with this person again. Your sign-off should be "warm," "facilitative," and/or "social" in nature. Add your full contact information as required.

HOW TO WRITE UP YOUR PROFESSIONAL REFERENCES

★ Note: Gone are the days when you would ask employers for *written* letters of recommendation.

This is another area in which it truly pays off to be prepared. In every job throughout your career, try to enlist one to three people to serve as "verbal references" for you. Invariably, once you are long gone from a given role, some of your references will have moved on, as well. You will always (read: eventually) need an "insider" to vouch for your work at past employment houses.

Here's a handy cheat sheet for what should be included in your references. Try to provide at least two to three "direct-report" references (read: bosses) and two or three "professional and/ or character references" (read: peers/colleagues) using the below format. The most important aspects of references are their *full contact information*, and the *context* in which you worked with this person.

List your references using this format:

[Name]

[Title]

[Organization]

[City, Province/State]

[Mobile number]

[Direct line]

[Email]

[Context] I reported [directly or indirectly] to [name] in [role] for [timeframe].

70

★ Three references aren't enough. When everything comes down to the wire and a recruiter/hiring manager is checking your references, having more options is good (rather than too few), to cover reference peeps who might be unreachable on short notice. I'd go as high as offering the hiring team five or six references.

KILLER APP ALERT—Reference ABCs! When advising your references that someone will be calling them regarding a job you've applied for, it's a great idea to **give them specific areas of the job description to focus on when referencing you**. Say the main requirements of the potential job are: a) project management; b) communication skills; and c) budgeting. Ask each of your references to focus specifically on a, b, *or, c*—i.e., have them highlight one area in particular. Once that's accomplished, they can then generally reference any other strengths they feel you have. That's another way in which your business case gets reinforced . . . via your references. Right?

Clever!

SOCIAL MEDIA PROFILES

LinkedIn is currently the most important social media platform as regards your career. Your LinkedIn profile should, ideally, mirror the content of your resume. Of course there are other industry or sector-specific platforms, like IMDB and their ilk. But LinkedIn is the current "go to" for everyone. Keep your "summary profile" to one or two paragraphs. Scrub it annually for consistency with your other marketing tools to ensure the content is current. Again, make it warm and friendly, as opposed to stiff or overly formal. Make sure your profile has full contact information. You don't want to miss any outreach frankly.

★ **Never underestimate the value of "recommendations" and "endorsements" on LinkedIn.** As a recruiter, I want to see that a solid number of professionals are giving you their personal backing (aka offering you "social proof"). Plentiful endorsements, and a small handful of written recommendations will stand you well. Offer your friends and colleagues endorsements too. What goes around comes around.

LANDMINE ALERT! Please note that LinkedIn, Facebook, Instagram, Twitter, etc., can make or break your career. If you're an adult and know the difference between right and wrong, you will know *not* to include any politically or morally incorrect messaging in your social-media profiles. Also, you will want to closely monitor just how *personal* you get on these platforms. Professionals are professionals. Don't represent yourself as any less.

E-MAIL "SIGNATURES"

KILLER APP ALERT—Email Signatures! Nothing is more frustrating to a hiring manager/recruiter than to have to dig for your contact information. It's not enough to have it listed on your resume. That just makes it my job to go find your resume (again). Your email signature should have your full name, title, and contact information—always. It should be included on every single email you send out. Look at it this way: Why would you lose a single opportunity to brand yourself? Hm? So brand yourself: Be forthcoming for your peers and let them know how to reach you on their platform of choice.

VOICE-MAIL MESSAGES—THE UNSUNG HERO OF MARKETING TOOLS

Use your full name, always. State it cleanly and clearly, and be sure both names don't run into each other—especially if you have an unusual or complicated name. Keep your voice-mail message short, and offer a timeline for a response. And honour it. At the barest minimum, update your voice-mail message annually. A true professional will update their voice mail anytime they are away from their desk for any extended period.

Check your voice-mail messages regularly, and *be sure to listen to them before you return someone's call.* Making someone repeat the message they just left you is mighty annoying. Especially to recruiters!

★ Don't answer calls unless you are in a position to do the caller justice. If it's not a good time to take a call, let them go to voicemail. But truly, don't let them go to voicemail where possible—make hay while the sun shines, as they say...

CHAPTER 10

10 WAYS TO BOSS YOUR JOB SEARCH

There's *so* much more to life than trolling for job postings . . .

For the record (and when you think about it), there really are only four ways to make money in life:

1. Securing a full-time, reduced-time, or part-time staff gig;

2. Offering your services and/or product as a freelancer (aka "a side-hustle");

3. Monetizing a hobby or talent you enjoy (for passive and/ or ad-hoc income); and

4. Securing a "survivor gig" – any thing part-time to drive income that allows you to pursue your goals around it. Enough said.

MINDSET ALERT—Financial diversification is key! Finance specialists will tell you that having a "diversified portfolio" is a healthy financial strategy. Applying that concept to your professional life is an equally smart and healthy strategy. Open up your mind, and think about diversifying your revenue streams. Think about driving income in multiple ways, including both direct *and* passive income. Write a book! ☺

Each of the above methods of making money has both advantages as well as disadvantages. **Staff jobs** are highly competitive, not to mention demanding. Full-time work is really tough to secure and maintain. Having a staff job with regular income is great—if you can get one. But also quietly building **freelance services** in the background or, putting together the framework for a small "side hustle" in your specialty area, is also a really smart plan. If you are unemployed, getting a **"survivor gig"**—retail, delivering things, virtual assistant, whatever—can literally save your financial reality while still allowing time within the rest of the week to devote to job-search in your industry of choice.

"Monetizing a hobby": Everyone in media who works with me knows that I am deeply involved in animal rescue and animal advocacy. Not just regular animals, but animals with medical, emotional, geriatric, and/or palliative issues. So by necessity through the years, I have built a lot of expertise around caring for frail and fragile animals. When I bought my home a number of years ago, I was concerned about being able to carry the mortgage, and was mindful of the coming transformation of Canadian media and its expected impact on my recruiting business. So I thought: Why don't I start a small boarding business on the side, taking care of other peoples' special-needs animals? It turned out to be one of the smartest moves I have ever made. I manage my special needs boarding business easily alongside my daytime recruiting/coaching business, as I work from a home office. And it has saved the mortgage more than once. So if you have a hobby you enjoy that you could take to the marketplace (product *or* service), by all means, do. Highly recommended! Establishing a side business does take time (approximately five years), but it is well worth it.

Takeaway: Diversification is key to keeping money rolling in.

Now, about that job search . . .

> " *People are motivated in different ways, and that is amplified in smaller companies. Research the ladder, up and down—how are the employees feeling? Is your boss a good person? How is the company doing? Get some insider information on what it's really like to work there.* "

—Jeffrey Elliott, chief executive officer
www.tablerockmedia.com

You will never go wrong if you do your research. Having said, that, it follows that *you will go wrong, if you don't do your research.* So do yourself proud and don't neglect your research.

Most people think that job search consists of just "online job search"—i.e., endlessly trolling the web for postings that match your particular skills and field. While it's a "good-enough/ reasonable" strategy, you really do not want it to be your main lifeline. Online job search, IMHO, is the least effective way to get a job, and is really just the tip of the iceberg when it comes to different methods of finding employment.

Stronger strategies for job searches include (and, I might add, go from lesser to greater importance/efficacy—the further down this "career activism" list you go). This is where the career activism rubber hits the road:

1. **Trolling the net for job postings** on large search engines and job boards, and applying online with a cover letter/cover email.

2. **Setting up "Google Alerts"** for jobs in your geo-local and/or functional area. It's best to get job postings delivered to your desktop, rather than spend a lot of valuable time searching for them.

3. **Bookmark the HR website pages** of companies you would like to join, and check them weekly for new postings. Once or twice a week is enough—job postings don't measurably change day over day, but likely *will* change week over week.

4. **Maintain a "Contacts Database"** to help track companies and stakeholders, and ensure your contacts database is constantly updated. LinkedIn is fine, but I prefer my own method to manage my contacts. I actually use a job-search spreadsheet (refer to Chapter 12's "The Hidden Job Market") to manage my contacts. I list companies in alphabetical order: I note the company mandate, the contacts I know within the company, and any other little bits of information I pick up. I regularly review my contacts database for opportunities to "touch base" with my contacts for potential business opportunities, or to do simple "marketing touchdowns" with them, just for the sake of remaining connected. Think of your contacts as "social equity." You need business contacts to explore business development and develop job leads. Not too little, not too much. Just touch base—keep the relationships and dialogue ongoing.

5. Ask **friends and colleagues** to make a point of finding out if any jobs are coming up (in your skills area) in their companies, and ask them to give you a heads up. Please understand that this is not a *light* or *informal* request. This is a direct ask! Ask specifically for their commitment to follow through with a little insider intel for you. There is no harm in making this request if you make it nicely. ★ Note: Only close friends and trusted colleagues, mind—not individuals who may be competitors in your field.

6. **Join LinkedIn groups** and participate in discussion boards to increase your visibility and engagement, and stay current on jobs and trends.

7. **"Offline job search" is key. This means networking:** At conferences, industry gatherings, events, meet-ups, lunch-and-learns, alumni groups, business groups, job fairs, seminars, etc. Check out an event you've never gone to before. Be present, circulate, increase your profile, and participate actively in your industry.

8. **Third-party introductions.** Getting a third-party introduction works wonders. It makes the recipient of your outreach "more accountable" to the third party, and the likelihood for their taking action on an introduction to you will be higher. Think of it this way: You can go in cold, or, you can go in with a stamp of approval from a friend/colleague. Door # 2 is definitely better. It's called "social proof" for a very good reason.

9. **Second-party referrals** also work well. When a friend or colleague tells you: "You should talk to [so and so] over at [company]," ask them directly to *refer you*.

Have them put their money where their mouths are—and not just pay you lip service. Referrals (usually done by email or LinkedIn) lend you more social proof—referrals offer critical context that makes you "less of a stranger" to one of their contacts. Of course, be sure your referral knows you will be calling the potential business lead. And when you do, be sure to mention and thank the person who referred you. It works like magic for getting someone's (reasonably favorable) attention! Then go in prepared with your "business case." Job searches are painful for everyone—not just you. And not just now. Pay it forward for others who find themselves in equally difficult job-search situations, and be sure to return the favor for your referral at a later date, when they might need you.

10. **Mentors & Learning Partners**: Honestly, if you don't have a mentor or professional "learning partner" whom you can reach out to for professional advice and critical introductions, you need to find one. Or two. Or three! Mentor relationships can be formal or informal, consistent or sporadic. **Mentors should always be at a more senior level than you.** You and your mentor can work out the rules. I've been fortunate enough to have two long-term, professional mentors (and a learning partner) spanning the last twenty to twenty-five years. Every time I've been in doubt about anything professionally, I've turned to them for counsel. They, and the practice itself, have served me exceptionally well.

Getting a "learning partner" at the same level as you is also a brilliant strategy. Choose a colleague from your industry/sector. A learning partner is a friend or colleague whom you can *implicitly* trust and turn to, when you are in doubt about any business-related issue. My learning partner happens to be a lawyer. I have turned to him time and again for counsel on all kinds of small business issues. He, in turn, has turned to me for counsel on recruiting strategies, labor market information, hiring protocols, etc. We met at a training conference some twenty years ago and decided to commit to always being there for each other. It's been a wonderful, truly beneficial, truly reciprocal relationship. (Shout out to Michael Steinberg—you rock, brother!)

> **"** *Have multiple mentors! Find established industry people or peers—have several people you can use as a sounding board. Relationships are key! I never appreciated how hugely important mentoring is. Two academic degrees are great, but without mentors to guide you, you can't know that you're doing the right thing.* **"**
>
> —Deanna Cadette, policy analyst
> **www.writersguildofcanada.com**

MINDSET ALERT! Your business contacts are your lifeline— you must maintain relationships with your business contacts throughout your entire career. When business contacts "back you," they are putting their professional names on the line for you. Do them proud. Bring your A-game to the equation by learning, growing, and developing in tandem with your peers. Don't just stand on your industry's sidelines—get in there and contribute to the cause! Find your tribe, and take your place amongst them. Last, be sure to give back. You must reciprocate, and you must deliver for friends and colleagues, too. Show them that you have their back, just as they have yours.

> **"** My best advice is to become a student of whatever industry or discipline you intend to follow in your career. Research it as thoroughly as you can, with a focus on the future, and where that industry is going next. Get to know the players and establish contact and relationships where you can. Study not only the specifics of the position or location you seek, but know the big picture. Read everything you can find.**"**

—Hudson Mack, veteran news director and anchor
www.harbourpublishing.com/title/HudsonMack

Consider all the time that you spend on social media. If you reduced that time by 25%, and devoted it to industry research instead, think about the *significant* difference that would make in your professional life!

KILLER APP ALERT—Schedule Goals and Job-Search Activities Weekly! Dedicate one half hour each and every week, to blocking off time in your calendar for various job search activities. You'll be amazed at how productive you can be if you take the time to block specific times off, for specific tasks. In the evening and on weekends, do yourself a favour and allow yourself time off from job search and financial worries. There's nothing meaningful you can do for job creation/financial revenue generation on weeknights and weekends. So take care of yourself and your life: Change your mind, get a break from it all, and then you will be ready to get back to job search on the following morning, or Monday morning, as the case may be. This is a classic example of "putting your own oxygen mask on first." Be this person!

HOW TO MANAGE YOUR WEEKLY JOB SEARCH /
LEAD DEVELOPMENT

MONDAY	TUESDAY	WEDNESDAY	THURSDAY	FRIDAY
1. Do online searches for job postings through aggregators like: Workopolis, LinkedIn, Charity Village, Indeed.ca, etc.	1. Job Applications & Cover Letters and emails . . . or writing business proposals.	1. Lead generation through cold calls & social media outreach.	1. By Thursday, anyone working in an office is reaching their saturation point and/or burn-out stage and will probably be too busy to return calls, so . . .	1. On Fridays, everyone is emotionally checked out of their jobs, so Friday is a great day for planning networking lunches, coffees . . .
2. Monitor and/or Bookmark the human resources/ job posting pages of companies you are interested in working with.	2. Use templated cover letter/emails and tailor to specific job postings.	2. Build LinkedIn contacts: invite others to connect. When they do, write back, thank them, and suggest a small "next step for a purposeful connection"	2. Best to keep Thursdays reserved for content creation for personal projects, or . . .	2. Great day to take care of admin chores!
3. Check relevant industry unions, and or guilds for job postings.	3.Review and/or scrub resume to include "keywords" from job posting	3. Work on getting "third party referrals" or introductions from friends	3. Build in time for creating marketing tools like your resume, bio, email signature, cover letter/ email templates, etc.	3. Book informal meetings and/or calls with mentors and/or learning partners.
4. Build "balance breaks" into your day at lunch and end of business.	4. Build "balance breaks" into your day at lunch and end of business.	4. Build "balance breaks" into your day at lunch and end of business.	4. Build "balance breaks into your day at lunch and at end of business.	4. Take the rest of the day off— you've earned it!
5. Evening networking events (as applicable)	5. Evening networking events (as applicable)	5. Evening networking events (as applicable)		

What about those "applicant tracking systems" that are screening your application(s)?

Larger companies usually have enough profit margin and high enough HR volumes to warrant using an "applicant tracking system" (ATS). These are computer programs that assess and screen an applicant's degree of match/suitability to a given job posting, through pre-programmed algorithms.

Hopefully at this point, you are "scrubbing" your marketing tools on an annual basis. I strongly encourage you to start new documents from scratch every two to three years. **Many people work with dated word-processing software and old resumes that have a bunch of legacy formatting** hidden in their background software that may not be compatible with (nor process-able through) larger companies' more current software packages. Something as simple as a resume over-loaded with out-dated software, or software formatting can jam an applicant tracking system! This could take you out of the running for a job—and you won't even know it!

Further, when applying to larger companies using ATS, be sure to review the job description and **incorporate some of the language, or "buzzwords" from the job description into your cover letter and your resume content.** You may think "client service" is good enough, but if the ATS system is looking for "customer relationship management" (even though they are largely the same thing), you need to tailor your application and resume accordingly (within reasonable means). That doesn't mean plagiarize . . . Just do your best to mirror the requirements of the job within your application package wherever possible.

Remember: If they ask you to state your expected range of compensation in your cover letter, be sure to give them a good wide spread. If they ask you to offer up your salary requirements, don't neglect to do so—omitting this information can take you right out of the running. (Reference Chapter 17's "Negotiating Your Salary and Deal Points.)

Larger companies usually have quite specific requirements to get through the ATS. Be sure to play by the rules.

Remember: HR and ATS are there to screen you out—your job is to get yourself screened in.

MINDSET ALERT! Don't spend a lot of time trying to figure out what's going on at a given company after you hit "send" on your application. Do your best with the system at hand, and then let it go. You will either hear from them or not. Pivot straight back to your job search and keep developing leads (read: get more eggs in your basket).

CHAPTER 11

HOW WELL CONNECTED ARE YOU?

It's not just about "who you know"—it's also about "how you work it."

★ Before we even get into networking best practices, please know that you cannot network properly unless you have first mastered:

1. How to shake hands;

2. How to introduce yourself; and

3. How to (properly) introduce other people to one another.

When in doubt, check out *How To Work A Room,* (revised edition) by Susan Roane.

Networking is a lifelong process. Building contacts is a must—and managing and leveraging those contacts consistently over time, is an art. I refer to it fondly as "social equity." "Equity" means money! If I've said it once, I've said it a thousand times: You cannot make money in isolation.

There are only two ways to network: online and offline. For the foreseeable future, LinkedIn will remain the social-media "go-to" platform for building connections online. Technically, LinkedIn is fine, and useful—but it's not the Holy Grail. There are many more social-media platforms that hiring managers are using. Networking at events and conferences or through alumni groups (aka "boots-on-the-ground/offline networking") is really the best way to go—as much, and as often, as you can.

> *I would underscore the power of networking, which is typically treated as a short-term activity. If you're looking at thirty to forty years of a career, it's easy to underestimate the longer-term value in the people you meet and the relationships you have. There are more benefits that you can get from your network—not just the immediate rewards of an event. It's a long game, and ongoing networking is the best return on your investment.*

—Andy Robling, vice-president, client development
www.hays.com

Networking is truly is a "long-game." Be mindful of this. You will thank yourself.

MINDSET ALERT! Many are aware that they need to network, yet they secretly view networking as a "disingenuous act." Helloooo, projection! Some think that networking is schmoozing for the sake of schmoozing. News flash—it's not. Others think that when networking, you have to pretend to be someone you're not. That's not the case, either. Everyone networks because they inherently know they cannot be successful in isolation. Get your head around the fact that you need others to succeed. We are an inter-dependent species. Think of networking as a simple process of making new business friends. It is solely a function of finding like-minded individuals in your shared communities of interest, and building rapport with them. It's called "social equity" (equity = money) for a very good reason.

Each and every contact you have has the potential to add to your income!

★ Don't kid yourself, **disingenuousness and insincerity are easily detectable,** even to a stranger. Don't be this person.

★ **Don't speak negatively** about your industry, the event, any participants at the event, your profession, your company, your colleagues, or your boss. *Ever.* It will come back to bite you later.

★ **Refuse to participate in gossip.** Take charge and redirect (or, better yet, *elevate)* the conversation when someone "goes there" with you. Discretion is always the better part of valour.

★ Tempting as it may be, **don't spend all your time at networking events with your friends.** You are there to meet new people.

KILLER APP ALERT—Plan for the Networking Event!
Research organizations whose events will specifically help boost your knowledge and contacts. If an organization's mandate or client base relates specifically to your goals, you will benefit from participating. You may choose to attend because you want to gain greater insight into your industry. Or, you want to meet a certain panellist or presenter who will

be there. Or, you just want to meet and hang with like-minded people to share career experiences. Whatever your reason, knowing and identifying all the participants is a part of the planning process.

★ **Never, ever, ever attend a networking event without a plan.** A big mistake that networkers make is neglecting to do their homework, by actually planning for attending an event. Do your research. You should know the names, roles, and organizations of various industry stakeholders who will be attending. Don't attend events just for the sake of attending. Make sure every event is the right fit for you, and that you have a concrete reason for being there. Stating why you're attending can be a great conversation starter!

No matter at what age or stage you are in your career, know that as an industry professional, **you have every right to belong at professional events.** Please consider yourself a card-carrying member of your own industry. Get there as early as you can, and make it a goal to meet as many people as possible.

Everyone is nervous at networking events—so try to make it easy on others. One way to feel comfortable is to act like a host . . . even if you are not hosting. Don't shy away from introducing individuals to each other, offering to get refreshments, and generally helping others feel at ease. Another way to increase your comfort level is by going prepared with a little industry "small talk." Read the business news that day and bring a little something to the conversation.

One of my favourite tactics is to identify someone who is alone and looking uncomfortable. Walk up, shake hands, and introduce yourself, telling them who you are, and letting them know why you're there. Believe me, they will welcome the company. Then, widen the circle by inviting others to join the conversation. In other words, be facilitative!

Keep your networking conversations to about five minutes each.

Meet, greet, repeat!

Offer your business card. Your conversation partners will immediately get theirs out to exchange with cards with you. ★ Don't have your business cards buried somewhere so that you have to dig for them.

It's appropriate to ask for referrals and introductions, but ★ don't aggressively ask about jobs or insider information on companies at a networking event. Save that for a later conversation, when you're a bit more of a "known entity."

Be authentic and use good manners. You are there to gather intel. Successful networkers understand that a first meeting is just the tip of the iceberg. Keeping track of the people you've met and finding ways to be helpful to them, *over time*, are the keys to success. You can let them know about relevant job opportunities that you are aware of, or, you can offer to introduce them to people you know. When you show that you are looking out for them, they will be much more amenable to helping you in return.

Post-networking follow-ups: Within a day or two of an event, go through the business cards you gathered and add their information into your contacts database for future reference. Make a note of what event you met at—that history always comes in handy down the road. Then, follow up with a short email letting them know you were glad to meet them. If you had a particularly meaningful connection with someone, reference it in your email. If you want to deepen the connection with someone, let him/her know it! A good way to further the conversation is to ask this person to let you know about upcoming events, and promise them the same in return. Everyone appreciates being in on what's happening—to say nothing of a legitimate excuse to reconnect. Find ways to reconnect already!

How often can you contact your industry connections? Drum roll: It's OK to contact someone when you have something *new* to bring to the table. Examples include: a new marketing piece you've put together (revised resume, demo reel, blog, etc.); an article you feel may be useful to them; news on industry trends; an invitation to an event; and/or a request for a critical introduction.

Or . . . be social and simply say hello. Sometimes I reach out just for the sake of reaching out—informally. I'll call someone and let them know I was thinking about them, and ask how they are. You'd be amazed at how much people like to be contacted for non-business reasons. Use your imagination, industry knowledge, and marketing tools—there are innumerable ways and reasons to connect with industry colleagues!

Remember: You didn't enter the world knowing how to network.

Neither did anyone else.

Networking is an art. You need to build the muscle.

I think the key piece to be aware of, is that we are all part of one network—a seemingly innocuous chance meeting. Each individual, colleague, employer, or organization becomes part of your network. Just as you are moving through your career life, so is everyone else. You never know where your paths may cross again. So don't scratch anyone off the list."

—Caroline Konrad, director, Career & Co-op Centre
  www.ryerson.ca

CHAPTER 12

THE "HIDDEN" JOB MARKET

What and where is the hidden job market?

MINDSET ALERT! Before we begin, I want to make an important distinction re: "job search." Most people refer to job search as exactly that: job search. But I break job search into two discrete functions: job search "research" and job search "strategy." Keep this in mind as you begin to build your job-search spreadsheet/contacts database.

The hidden job market is made up of all the available jobs that never get posted online. They are job opportunities that are quietly networked one person at a time, verbally, within a community of peers. And there are plenty of those jobs out there—your task is to find them! So what's the trick? Answer: Researching connections! The more research you do, and the more companies and people you explore, the more you will find out. It just makes sense, right?

As un-sexy as it is, I break my lead-development (read: job-search research) information down into five columns on an Excel spreadsheet (aka my "contacts database"). **Excel spreadsheet + company and stakeholder information = contacts database.** I gather all the intel I can on the companies that make up my industry, and park it all in one spreadsheet. Working a spreadsheet in "columns" (per breakdown below) is the best way to harness career activism:

1. Track companies;

2. Track company mandates;

3. Track business units (aka departments) and the various stakeholders therein;

4. Flesh out your business case; and

5. Plan your "marketing touchdowns" to get in front of the right people, at the right time, for the right reasons. Building your knowledge, contacts, and intel on the company, will get you a lot closer to that job offer than *not* doing so.

Note: Whichever platform you use to track your business leads, make sure it has a long shelf life with up-to-date software, and that the data are compatible with export programs (like email aggregators, etc.).

MINDSET ALERT: "A-List" Companies v. "B-List" Companies: ★ Don't target your "A-list" companies until you have done a bunch of trial runs with "B-list" companies. Get some job-search practice by focusing first on the companies that you are merely interested in, i.e., "B-list," before going after your prime "A-list" targets. Most people target their "A-list" companies first—which is a huge mistake, because they're not ready yet (read: un-rehearsed). When I coach recent media grads on job search, I ask them to apply to ten local health centres. And they're like: "But I don't want to work in the health sector." And I answer: "Exactly!" Of course, they're not really going to do it. But it makes the point that you need to practice on companies you're not overly invested in before targeting the companies that you are seriously invested in. Get some practice. Hone your pitch.

Here's *why* you want to maintain a seemingly super un-sexy Excel job-search spreadsheet/contacts database:

1. Knowledge is power;

2. Mandate and stakeholder information are *gold*;

3. All the info you need on a given company is at your fingertips, searchable in a nanosecond in your database; and

4. You'll have a ready-made business case sitting right there in your notes with which to impress somebody, command their attention, and convince them that you are better prepared than anyone else. Because you *are* better prepared than anyone else! Trust me. *Your Excel contacts database is your new BFF!*

Here's *how* to build out your "job search spreadsheet":

Column 1: Most people make their databases searchable by individual last names. I, however, suggest you **list the companies** you would like to work with **in alphabetical order** on your spreadsheet. Your list will *theoretically* contain two types of companies: Those that you would die and go to heaven to work with (aka "the A-List"), and those you are merely interested in (aka "the B- List"). The reason you build your list alphabetically by company, is to research a given company and its mandate *first*, to help you decide if you even want to work with them in the first place. After that, you research the "team players." Team players IMHO are less important than mandates. You need to be "bought into" what the company is doing *before* entertaining working with them. After all, you want to be making the decisions on where you want to work and why. That just makes sense, right? Put yourself in charge of the process from the get-go.

Column 2: Notes, notes and more notes! Note the **company mandate.** Review the "About Us" page of their website along with any recent news releases or digital press on them. Note the **services and/or products** they're providing, the **markets** they serve, and *why*. Note any **new business directions** on the "news" page of their site—anything you can review quickly before a phone call to keep you current on the company's role and its successes within its own industry. I try to add one note per year on each company in my database, to stay current on their mandates and be able to impress them with my knowledge of them. Works like a charm!

Column 3: Identify the name of the business unit (aka the department) in the company you want to do business with. It could be the executive team, human resources, finance, or marketing department—whichever business unit your skills are best suited to. Then **research stakeholders within that business unit** on LinkedIn. Look (primarily) for decision-makers, but also (secondarily) for any stakeholders you might know via a third party. The goal is to build your knowledge of the team, as well as to build/increase your exposure to that team.

Column 4: The next column will give you the opportunity to **draft a "business case,"** tailored to each specific company. I cannot stress this enough—ask yourself these four questions:

Why you? Why would this company want to hire you? What's unique about you?

Why now? How does this fit into your professional goals and/or plan?

What role do you want to play with this company?

Why do you want to work with this company in particular?

I fondly refer to making a business case as my "brain candy".

> **"** *When teaching my students why they need to understand what a business case is and how critical it is in designing their new business idea, I always encourage them to know what questions they need to answer. If they truly put the work into designing a business plan, these questions will be answered—all of them. Good or bad. One has to have a script, and be able to pitch it. On paper. In person. And most importantly, own it in their head.* **"**

—Tara Jan, executive producer

KILLER APP ALERT! This "Business-Case Formula" is a multi-purpose tool: "Why you, why now, why this role, why this company"? You can use your answers to these questions to close out your cover letter and/or script your phone calls. You can also use it while networking, or during the course of an interview. You can use it as your exit and entry positioning statements (refer to Chapter 18's "How to Start Your New Job on the Right Foot"), or, use a shorter, "mini-version" in your follow-up thank-you note after an interview or a business development meeting. That's why I call it "brain candy." If

I'm calling you, you can bet I have a business imperative in mind, and using this formula, I'm able to state my business case relatively easily, and stay on message with my business priorities—aka "get your ask together."

Column 5: "Marketing Touchdowns": Last but not least, make notes in a final column regarding the dates and times you have contacted anyone at that company, and how it went. Jot down any points of the discussion you had in your contacts database. In this column, I also plan my next steps (aka "marketing touchdowns"). If you have these notes in your database, the next time you call or email this person, you can handily reference where you left off from your spreadsheet, and tie it into a new idea, or a new call to action. I don't see reaching out to a company as a "finite" or "incremental" exercise, but rather as an ongoing process of relationship building, and (more importantly) trust building. I put some time into planning when I'm going to contact them next, and the context I plan to reference/use in my approach. The goal here is to build your exposure to the team, however long it takes. Psych 101 would call it "increased opportunities for positive interaction"—aka "marketing touchdowns." Brilliant!

Memorize this: Job search is a process of relationship- and trust-building.

Once my contacts database is populated with basic information, I **cycle through the companies and stakeholders on an intermittent** basis and review where I left off with them. Then, I try to find new reasons to reach out, touch base, and get my name in front of each of them again (without being annoying). I reach out for specific reasons, and offer a clear call to action—usually two to three times a year. And then I just keep adding more companies and people to my database.

My company is called mediaINTELLIGENCE.ca for a darned good reason!

Once trust has been built with any given contact, I have always believed that there isn't any harm in making a polite inquiry about potential upcoming work. Think on that for a minute. A simple, polite inquiry like: "Is there a chance you have any insight into upcoming hires in [company name]'s [+department] that you might share with me? They will either share or they won't. And whether or not they share depends on how long and how trusting your relationship is. The more companies and contacts you have on your spreadsheet, the greater the chances of uncovering an upcoming role. It's a numbers game. The more trusting the relationship, the more they are likely to share.

What if they don't have any upcoming roles? That's fine—thank them politely and ask if it would be appropriate for you to check back in three or six months down the road. Sooner or later, they are going to need a new role filled in your skills area, and you'll be primed for consideration because you'll have positioned yourself as "top of mind."

Reality Check: How many times do you think this recruiter has been asked to "keep [person] in mind for upcoming roles"? Oh, dear . . . That is one of the silliest statements you could ever make, no offence! When you ask someone to keep you in mind, you are making it their responsibility to remember you, when in fact, it is your responsibility to stay top of mind with them. Think about that. How do you stay top of mind, you ask? Short answer: Strategic marketing touchdowns.

MINDSET ALERT: Authenticity Rules. Try to look at job-search strategy this way: If you've gone to all the trouble of researching companies, their mandates and stakeholders, and scripting your outreach and delivering your message as politely and concisely as possible, *why would they not take you seriously*? It's the un-prepared/disorganized job seekers that are truly off-putting. Now, you might not always be responded to, but your level of preparedness will speak volumes. After that, it's either a yes or a no. That's business—it's not personal.

★ Never be the person who calls up and says something like "Um, can you tell me a little bit about your company? My standard reply is: "Can you read a website?"

What if you don't know who and where the companies are in your industry? Good question. Let's go there, too: For any industry—be it finance, government, health sector, media, you name it—there is a trade association that guides it, binds it, and/or brings it together. So whichever industry you are targeting for work, **find out who the associations/ organizations are that hold annual conferences or events for that industry**. Because any companies that attend or participate in (sector-specific) conferences and events wouldn't be participating if they weren't financially healthy enough to pay the price of admission in the first place. This means they have money. It follows that if they have money to attend conferences, they have money to pay staff. A good sign! Even better: Conferences will always promote their industry partners on their event website pages. And those industry partners (companies + delegates from those companies) are your new "job-search shopping list"—tailored specifically to the industry you want to work in.

Cool, eh?

So do your research. It's *so* worth it! Knowledge is a real confidence booster. Get those companies into your contacts database, make notes on their mandate/mission, research the business unit that applies to you and its' internal stakeholders, draft up your "business case", and start planning your marketing touchdowns. They will be impressed with your knowledge, as well as your diligence. And because you have done the research, your confidence will be at an all-time high, and you will be twice as prepared as any of your competition.

Even cooler.

> *Expect that there will be detours along the way. It's important not to waste any time on a career path or in a job that isn't getting you where you want to go, doing what you want to do. I stayed in jobs longer than I would have, trying not to appear to be job-hopping, and to show that I was a stable person. And there's value in all of that—but I would tell my younger self, once it's apparent something isn't working, to leave that job and find something better. If it's not working out, there's no point in postponing the inevitable.*

—Alisyn Camerota, CNN anchor
www.alisyncamerota.com
www.cnn.com/shows/new-day

CHAPTER 13

HOW TO GO FROM "STRANGER" TO "YOU'RE HIRED!"

Now, let's drill down on those "marketing touchdowns."

MINDSET ALERT: Job search is a process! It's hard to break through to people you don't know, and it's harder still to get past applicant-tracking systems. But there are many practical ways to improve the success rate on your outreach. The trick is to maintain your job-search *research* on an ongoing basis—i.e., it is not a finite exercise! You apply once, don't hear back, feel rejected, and never try again. Sound familiar? If you take a *finite approach*, you are doing yourself a tremendous disservice. The magic lies in focus and persistence.

It's a seemingly universal thing that people fear, or at least suspect "l'étranger." And I find that to be a particularly sad reality . . . In my worldview, business inquiries should be welcomed amongst professionals. But not everyone is a true professional. If you approach someone who doesn't know you and you don't offer any context for your outreach, your inquiry can easily fall off his/her desk. They will ask themselves: "Who is this person and why should I care?" So give them a reason to care by offering them a little (relevant) context.

As previously mentioned, it is always **best to approach unknown colleagues with an introduction from a third-party** (peer or colleague) you both know, or, to get a referral from a friend who is willing to lend their name to help you forge a connection with someone new in your network.

That said, sometimes you need to go in cold. Some people try once, twice, three times to get hold of a person in their network, but don't get any response. And (by rights) they feel dissed. I couldn't tell you how many times I have heard industry people complain: "Well, I applied to [company] three times and I never heard back." Job search (and/or business development) literally requires a *series* of "marketing touchdowns" to get in front of the right person, at the right time, for the right reasons (refer to Chapter 12's "The Hidden Job Market").

KILLER APP ALERT—Marketing Touchdowns "Breakdown": Most calls and emails I receive are from someone who may be interested in my services (touchdown #1). So I respond/follow up and we have "a chat" (touchdown #2). I try to figure out what their needs are and usually recommend a concrete action—like sending them a link to the goals exercise on my website via email (touchdown #3). Usually, the person is intrigued enough to do the exercise (it's free!). So, I encourage them to send the results to me, along with a copy of their resume, so that I can review and provide feedback (touchdown #4). I follow up again by email with my comments on their resume, and offer some concrete advice on how to move forward on their goals (touchdown #5).

Slowly, they learn to put aside their automatic distrust, and we further the conversation. This *series of inquiries and responses* can take place over phone calls, emails, Skype, LinkedIn, even Facebook Messenger. And by the time the fourth or fifth marketing touchdown takes place, we are no longer strangers. As a result, **we have officially moved from "perfect strangers" to "known entities."** Progress!

The one thing I know for sure is that the business transaction is not going to happen or be finalized, over the first call or two. The relationship needs to be nurtured, and I need to continue to bring value, new ideas and information to the table in each interaction. Every exchange helps build trust and strengthen the relationship, while I secure their ongoing interest.

The same concept applies to job-search strategy à la career activism! All relationships need to be nurtured. You need to orchestrate a small handful of inquiries/topics that give you the opportunity to interact—aka "increased opportunities for positive interaction". You can start by simply reaching out to connect over LinkedIn **(touchdown #1)**. Don't be shy to connect: it is exactly what the LinkedIn platform was designed for. If they respond, be sure to thank them **(touchdown #2)**. Keep the thanks relatively benign, brief and social. Then, give the relationship a little time to sink in. A week or two later, try sending along some industry intel, or notice of an event, or an article, and then **gently nudge the exchange toward "next steps."** Next steps could be sending them your resume, or, asking for some insight into the company's hiring processes/culture, or, extending an invitation to an industry event **(touchdown #3)**, or, sending along an article or news piece you think would interest them. If they respond, this is **touchdown #4!** Just take baby steps, and let time work its magic. Think of "marketing touchdowns" as "landing a plane"—the wheels have to hit the ground a few times before they stick. Makes sense!

You are moving from "stranger" to "known entity." The "magic" of marketing touchdowns lies in the quality, authenticity, and timing of your interactions. Remember, it's a process!

A Note on "Professionals": In my experience, professionals return their calls, respond to emails, and further the business conversation. Professionals intrinsically understand the value of making and maintaining contacts and information sharing. By their very nature, professionals "facilitate" for each other. That is what they do. If they don't, I argue, they are not terribly professional—wouldn't you agree? So, if someone doesn't respond to you, or doesn't respond appropriately, take that as a sign that you might not actually want to do business with them because they are not actually professionals!

Honesty + accountability = respect. It's a two-way street! Finding your professional tribe is an epic marathon (not a sprint). But *so* worth it!

A Note on "Professionalism": ★ Don't be shy to take your rightful place professionally. You can be an entry-level professional, a mid-management professional, or a senior-management professional. But by all means, *own being a professional, and own being part of your professional community*. You need not ask for permission to belong—you already do. Your education and/or work experience automatically allow you to be a card-carrying member in your professional circles. Remember that.

> **"** Take the opportunity to get involved with activities related to, but outside of, your immediate company. Work on an industry task force. Learn. Meet people. Take the time to get involved in extra-curricular activities. Mentor, and be mentored—that's just hugely invaluable to you individually. **"**

—Andy Robling, vice president, client development
www.hays.ca

CHAPTER 14

WHAT MESSAGE ARE YOU PUTTING OUT THERE?

Managing your professional messaging is critical. Earlier, I wrote at length about how to set up your professional marketing tools to ensure that they represent you properly, and that they are in keeping with constantly evolving market best practices.

But there is much more to "marketing yourself" than meets the (literal) eye. You need to manage your message in *real time,* as well. That means from first impressions through to long-term relationships! Each and every exchange you have with industry colleagues matters over the long-term, and is a piece of the larger puzzle. Every exchange is an opportunity to manage your professional message, verbally, or in written correspondence. The short story is that you are messaging your community in *everything* that you do. So it follows that it would make sense to stop every now and again and take a good long look at how you are presenting to the outside world.

The same level of preparation goes into *scripting* your initial conversations to ensure that you stay on point. Rehearse those scripts out loud—and often! When you're doing outreach to strangers, **it makes perfect sense to *plan* your call**. Be sure you have thoroughly researched the company's website. You don't want to be asking any questions to which the answers are clearly available on a company's website.

And, plan the *timing* of the call. Make sure that you are not taking more than five to ten minutes of anyone's time. You're not going to call a key decision-maker in a news department at five p.m., right? You don't actually want to send an email at eleven p.m., do you? Do you really think you're going to get through to someone on the phone at three p.m. on a given business day? If there's a giant industry conference the first week of June, are you going to try to reach someone that week? Doesn't make sense. It is just bad form—and these details get noticed. I prefer calls at the very start of business, when I am fresh, and not yet caught up in the madness of a given business day, or, calls at the very end of business when I can breathe again. Note: Between 5:00-6:00 PM is always a good time to get hiring managers on the phone. Usually at end of business, executives are much more inclined to answer their own phones, as by then their assistants have gone home, and business has largely shut down for the day.

LANDMINE ALERT! A note about being "so busy": Please do not be the person who constantly talks about how busy they are. Reality check: everyone's busy! Busy needs no introduction! Busy is not special. It doesn't deserve heightened focus, because by constantly stating how busy you are, you may well undermine your own organizational capacity, and, you're sending the message that your professional life is not exactly under control. You really do not want to project this image.

KILLER APP ALERT: Manners! *Manners, simply put, can work miracles.* Work those miracles! "Please." "Thank You." "Thanks for your time." "I trust this is helpful." "Thanks for your kind consideration." "Sincerely appreciated." ★ Never, ever, ever, ever fail to use good manners. Being humble and grateful, are always well received.

The key points to message in your call are:

1. Right out of the gate, **thank them** for their "generosity of spirit in taking your call", and assure them you know that their time is valuable. This will show your respect for their time and expertise (which will pre-dispose them to liking you).

2. **Plan/script an introduction** you're comfortable with, that includes your full name and offers some "context" for the call. If you were referred through a friend or colleague, state it. If you're interested in employment with the company, or looking to participate in [x], state it.

3. **Give them a bit of information on yourself**—but don't go off the rails! If you have written up your profile statement, this is a great place to use it. (Refer to Chapter 8's "Resume Content/How to Write Your Professional Profile.")

4. Find a way to **introduce in your business case** that will tell this person why they might want to give your request serious consideration. Assure them of your keen interest in their company and impress them with your thoughtful planning. Don't worry about being nervous—they will expect you to be. Their comfort level with you will substantially increase the more organized and prepared you are, even if you are a

bit hesitant and make any slight flub. (Read: you're human . . . and so are they!)

5. Then, **make a clear ask.** "I was hoping you could answer a question or two regarding best practices for getting serious consideration for a job within your company." Or: "I was wondering if you could direct me to the appropriate decision-maker in [department] for potential employment with [company]." If they do give you a name, this is just excellent, because then you can introduce yourself to that decision-maker with: "[So and so] directed my inquiry to you." This makes them accountable to their colleague, and therefore more likely to give you their concentrated attention and more likely to give you further direction.

6. After "making your ask", they can respond with darned near anything, so it's tough to script. **They will offer some feedback on your inquiry**, and this is where you need to pay very close attention to what they recommend. You may have another question regarding that feedback. Or not. If not, re-affirm their feedback, and . . .

7. Thank them again for his/her time, and **ask if you might follow up by sending a copy of your resume to them via email.** Only a heartless person would say "no." Research their email formats before the call, and then just confirm their email address format is name.name@company.domain. They will be impressed once again by your preparedness.

8. Close out your call by mentioning that you hope to meet them one day, so that you might shake their hand

and thank them in person. They will note (and probably truly appreciate) your good manners, even if it never happens. Mind you, if you're a smart networker, you'll make a point of introducing yourself at an industry event, and making that personal thank you happen! (Yay! More opportunities for marketing touchdowns— Refer to Chapter 12's "The Hidden Job Market.")

You'll be amazed how much you can up your game if you just *plan* your script and *rehearse* your business case for each job lead—before you make that phone call.

Key messaging in your correspondence is just as important as it is in making phone calls. *Draft* your correspondence. Write a brief introduction, clearly state the nature of your outreach, and give them a clear "call to action" – ask them specifically for suggestions for next steps. When you give them a call to action is a good time to use their first name. It personalizes the exchange. Then, go over your correspondence, and edit it down as much as possible for brevity. Make sure there is adequate "white space" so that the email is not a chore to read. Scrub your salutation and sign off to ensure it is warm and social. I draft up all my correspondence, and let it sit overnight. I review crucial emails one last time first thing in the morning, before I hit "send".

> **"** *Learn to think and analyze. Learn to wait ten seconds before speaking. If you don't, you end up with a knee-jerk response. When you're just starting out, think before you speak.* **"**

—Colette Watson, senior vice president
www.rogers.media.com

CHAPTER 15

CAN YOU MAKE THE SHORTLIST?

Dilemma: You have applied for a lot of jobs, but are not getting any calls for interviews. It's likely the culprit is "lack of appropriate self-screening."

A job posting comes up. You give it a quick look—it's in your "field" so you jump on it and send in an application. That is what most people do, and that is why a given HR department gets hundreds of resumes for one job posting.

★ When applicants neglect to "crunch" the requirements of a job description, they are contributing to the problem of mass applications. If you *think* you're qualified, you only *think* it. If you crunch the job description, however, you'll *know* that you're qualified. So please, do yourself and human resources proud, and crunch that job description!

Here's a cool way to figure out if you should apply for a job that's posted:

KILLER APP ALERT—How to make the shortlist! Roughly seventy percent of candidacies are irrelevant due to lack of proper self-screening. However, when you see a job posting that's of interest to you, and you take five minutes to "do the math" (aka "crunch" the job description), you will definitely increase your interview call back rates. These simple steps will ensure that you are *actually qualified*, which will bolster your confidence in applying. It will also show the hiring manager that you've gone one step further than most candidates in determining your suitability to the job. It only takes a few minutes—you can avoid all kinds of heartache with this five-minute exercise. Who knew?

Here's how it's done:

Step 1. Print up the job description and get a coloured pen.

Step 2. Go to the "job requirements" or "required qualifications" section of the job posting.

Step 3. Review the first requirement. Let's say they want you to have five years' experience doing [x] for [y] market. You give it some thought, and you agree that you have [x] years' experience working in that role, in that market. So you assign yourself 100% on that requirement. Good start!

Step 4. Now, do that individually for *each* ensuing hard- and soft-skills requirements—simply **assign a "percentage of match" that you feel is appropriate to each requirement of the job.** Go through each one reasonably quickly and write down the percentage of match that resonates with you/your gut. Even if you have a lower percentage, like twenty or forty or even fifty percent on any one of the requirements, that's OK—because you will now know where your deficiencies lie. Knowing your deficiencies, you can then come up with a way to positively address them with the hiring manager in person, and/or, defend it in your cover letter, or in a screening call. *And no candidate is perfect: know this.* Very seldom does any one person have a hundred-percent match to the required skills.

The trick is to identify your strengths, minimize your deficiencies, and prepare a solution or defence, for your deficits.

On the other hand, **if you assign yourself a hundred percent for every requirement** (or almost every requirement) you may be fooling yourself by over-inflating your degree of match. This is why you are encouraged to take the time to see what your gut tells you regarding each individual requirement.

Step 5. When you get to the bottom of the list of required skills, **average it out!**

If you score over eighty-five percent, by all means send in your application. You will fall into the "strong maybe" or "yes" screening piles—depending, of course, on the competition (i.e., how your skills stack up against those of all the other applicants).

★ **Don't fudge the numbers**—just realistically assess your match to each skill, and crunch your overall average. If you come in at eighty-five percent, *you know most of the job, and still have room to grow in the role.* This can give you additional confidence writing your cover letter—let them know just how strong your match is! Feel free to state in your cover that you have done some analysis on the role and, in your humble opinion, you feel your match is [x] percent. Hiring managers will appreciate your diligence.

If you come in under eighty percent, carefully consider whether (or not) you want to apply. You will probably be outcompeted by those with a stronger overall skills match. Under eighty percent, you fall into a category where it's going to take some convincing in your cover letter/email and/or your screening call to be considered for an interview. Although, I must say, I've applied to something more than once that I was less than eighty percent on, and have still gotten serious consideration—because I've perfected how to make my "business case". With my business case in hand, I'm quite comfortable discussing *how* I am the best possible candidate for a given job, and *why*.

Doing this simple "Are you shortlist-able?" exercise will save you so much demoralization in your job search! It will prevent you from wasting your own time, and wasting hiring managers' time. It will also prevent you from feeling dejected in your job search due to not getting call backs. If everyone would simply do this exercise before applying for jobs, it would prevent the kind of scenario where tons of (under-qualified) people apply for the same job . . . not to mention probably help raise the GDP! This trick is worth its weight in gold.

When you "crunch" your percentage of match to each skill listed in the requirements section of a job posting, you significantly increase your chances of being called to interview. Be this person! It only takes a few minutes. You'll thank yourself. And the HR world will thank you, too.

" *Look on this as an exciting period in your life. Everything you are doing is about learning and exploring in the truest sense, and discovering what makes you tick, professionally. Think equally about the type of life you are looking to build. Your professional experiences will inform your overall life journey. Recognize that every step is about putting a piece into that larger puzzle—all part of the bigger journey that you are building over time.* **"**

—Caroline Konrad, director, Career & Co-op Centre
  www.ryerson.ca

CHAPTER 16

MASTERING THE INTERVIEW

Q: What are the three biggest mistakes you can make regarding an interview?

★ **Mistake #1: You don't do your research on the company mandate, and all of its stakeholders.** It is imperative to find out *what* the company does, and *why*. Research should include who is on the team, what their corporate culture is like, and what product or service they provide, and what audiences or markets they serve. *And why.* If you want to be a super-pro, check out their current (read: recent three months) news releases.

★ **Mistake #2: You don't spend time rehearsing your answers to questions about your skills—*out loud!*** For each job requirement, you need to make a statement that tells your recruiter: How long you did [role/skill], where you did it [company], and how well you did it [key successes]. Have I mentioned that you need to rehearse these answers out loud, LOL? If you only rehearse your answers in your head, you might as well fold your cards right now. Rehearsing out loud, in real time, transfers "random thoughts" from short-term to long-term memory. You don't want to just "think through the process"—you want to be able to rely on long-term memory, and truly prepared responses. Think about it: *Isn't your future worthy of just that little bit of extra preparation?* As in, your entire future v. ten minutes of your life, right now? Hm?

★ **Mistake #3: You don't make a "business case"** for your candidacy. By now, you should know this formula by heart!

Reality Check: Within seconds of meeting—in person, on the phone, or otherwise—you are perceived to be [x] or [y]—i.e., "categorized." Humans are lazy. They ascribe labels and/or make assumptions about you and your behaviours, simply because it's the easiest thing to do. The "label" (positive or negative) they assign you will become their default position on you—they will forever carry that first impression. They just don't take the time to analyze the *context* of any given situation. (I'll refrain from digressing into a full rant about the "fundamental attribution error." The FAE permeates society, and not in a good way. You would be well advised to acquaint yourself with it—it was a life-changing concept for me that really helped explain how so many people can be so damned judgmental and myopic about others . . .) (OK, I digressed a bit.)

So how do you present in an interview? Are you under or over-confident? Are you positive or negative? Are you secure or insecure? Are you easy-going, or overly formal? Are you a "nudge-nudge, wink-winker," telling jokes all the time? Do you talk non-stop (like I do) because you don't know how to handle silence? Or are you focused, pleasant, open, welcoming, facilitative, kind, calm and professional? These characteristics don't only come across in person, but on paper and in digital profiles, too. What you convey can be *so* easily misinterpreted by others!

MINDSET ALERT: Understanding the fact that *we are all subject to categorizing each other*, please bring openness and inclusivity to every professional action you take. You know, the golden rule: do unto others. We all want and need a kinder, more civil, and nurturing reality.

KILLER APP ALERT—Knowledge is Power! Knowledge gives you confidence. When you augment your knowledge, you automatically feel, and are, more on your game. If you want to build your business acumen beyond your particular craft or service, *study your industry*. Study its trends by reading professional white papers and industry forecasts, or signing up for information alerts in your field of business. Join an association that provides services to your industry. Join a board of directors, or a steering committee. The more you know, the more valuable you are to potential employers. So make life-long learning a top priority in your career. Increasing networking, public speaking, and presentation skills are all great ways to learn how to build your personal-messaging strengths.

Knowledge will always put you at the front of the line. Be part of the solution. Or, as one of my former bosses put it: "Professionals bring answers to the table, not questions."

> **❝** *A wise piece of advice I got from a former producer: "Remember this: when it comes to the selection of people for different positions, you need to understand that almost all decisions in terms of personnel are subjective. If they're looking for someone with green eyes and red hair, and you have blue eyes and brown hair, you're not getting the job. There are some positions where they go in a different direction, and you have to be prepared for that.* **❞**

—David Onley, senior lecturer
www.utoronto.ca

WHAT TO EXPECT IN A SCREENING CALL

These days, companies are likely to organize a "screening call" prior to asking you in to interview. Be prepared by having a Skype account and/or the ability to use FaceTime/Messenger or Google Hangouts. It could just be a phone call—but face to face, even over the Internet, is infinitely better. Whatever platform you use for a screening call, recruiters are looking for a few specific things:

Thing 1: They want to know if you hit the top educational and skills requirements of the job.

Thing 2: Through the course of your conversation, you are assessed for "cultural fit." They are gaging, by virtue of how you present to them and handle the conversation, whether they think you would be a good fit for their company. So, prior to the call, look into the company culture, its mission, and its "corporate social responsibility" (ongoing commitments to community initiatives and causes). Strive to be able to tie any or all of these company aspects into your business case!

Thing 3: They will want to know what "salary range" you are seeking. Best to be prepared to state an annual or weekly salary *range* (Refer to Chapter 17's *"Negotiating Your Salary and Deal Points")*.

Thing 4: They will ask about your "current availability." Understand that this is not a job offer! It is a simple question: Are you available immediately, or, do you need to give notice (and, if so, how much notice)? ★ Be careful not to read more into things than are actually there. Don't jump to any conclusions.

A screening call is usually allotted an approximate 10-15 minute window. The caller may or may not give you information on next steps (but you can always ask). Try hard to get the person's full name, title, and contact information, when possible. And get that info into your contacts database.

Have you heard about group interviews yet?

A new trend amongst employers is putting together a list of suitable candidates and inviting them all to interview at the same time. No pressure, right?

This is a very cost-effective way for employers to interview, but damnably intimidating for job seekers. If you rise to the challenge by doing your research on the company, rehearsing your answers to questions about the top skills requirements and preparing your business case, you will definitely outperform your peers—because most people still don't do their "interview homework" (refer to mistakes one to three, above). This is where rehearsing your answers really pays off. It's really important to rehearse and "stay on message" regarding your skills in preparation for a group setting. Make your words count. Invest in yourself by preparing. If you prepare, it will guarantee you make a stronger showing vis-à-vis your peer group.

PANEL INTERVIEWS

Sometimes (typically with larger companies), you will attend interviews in front of entire teams of decision-makers. It could be anywhere from two to five people, all of whom have a say in the hiring decision. From their standpoint, it's efficient to have all the inter-departmental team members involved in the hire attend, rather than stage several different interviews to accommodate them. Your future direct report will be there. Maybe even their boss, and probably an HR person. There may be another person or two from inter-disciplinary departments. These people are called "stakeholders" for a reason. They have a major stake in your hire. So, listen carefully to them all, and try to understand and address their particular concerns. Realistic or not, each of these people expects to have their individual needs addressed. The ability to actively listen, and to paraphrase individual concerns are critically important soft skills.

INTERVIEWS OVER COFFEE, LUNCH, OR DINNER

★ This is where things can get messy. You don't want to be inept in a social setting. Being prepared pays off: **brush up on your etiquette!**

Google the venue and menu, and know what to expect. ★ You don't want to spend a lot of time trying to figure out what is on the menu—especially, if you're veggie or vegan (yay!) or on any kind of restricted diet (boo!) Find out in advance what you can eat there, so that you don't waste a lot of time fussing over your order, and can smoothly get down to business.

Coffee: Implies an informal, short "informational" interview—they are checking you out for cultural fit and personal style. This is an opportunity to take your relationship to the next level. Anticipate thirty to forty-five minutes—if it goes to an hour, that's a good sign! But be sure not to overstay your welcome.

Lunch: Implies a fairly decent degree of interest and investment of their time in you. Lunch is usually an hour—it may go as long as an hour and a half, but that's max! ★ Don't be responsible for an out-of-control interview that goes way too long. If you are ordering coffees after your meal, be sure to check with the decision-maker to see if they have time remaining for coffee. Courteous gestures like that are always appreciated.

Dinner: **OK, now we're getting serious.** If they are investing in dinner with you, there is probably a serious, *senior-level* job under consideration or on offer. Know this, and recognize that dinner is an opportunity for them to get to know you on a deeper, more social level. Enjoy it! Dress well and be on time. The focus of a dinner meeting is social, and displaying good etiquette is paramount. Balancing a social medium with business is an art. The more of it you do, the better you get at it—if you need practice, attend breakfast lunch or dinners at conferences ★ Mind any drinking if you indulge. Don't get too comfortable.

In each case, try to walk away with some sense of their "next steps," as in: "Is it possible for you to share the timing of this hire with me?" Or: "Can you share the process on this hire going forward?" . . .You may get a subsequent referral to another internal stakeholder, a timeline on a potential upcoming job, or be given the opportunity to send them along some work samples that may help boost their team's interest in you and your skills.

Send a thank-you note at 9:00 AM sharp the next business morning to the hiring manager, and cc: all relevant stakeholders. Include a "mini-version" of your business case, to reinforce your suitability to the role, as well as your continued interest in their company.

Always remember that a deal isn't a deal until it's a deal.

HOW TO PREPARE FOR A FIRST-ROUND INTERVIEW

1. **Logistics**: Get all details on the date, time, location, and names of each participant—especially the decision-maker. Find out how much time they have allotted for the interview. It's very helpful to know this in advance so you can manage your time accordingly. Be prepared to handle an interview over video platforms, in case they want to screen you remotely.

2. Always **keep a copy of the job description** as reference.

3. **KILLER APP ALERT—How to Answer Interview Questions:** The best way to prepare answers to interview questions regarding your skills is by going through each individual requirement listed on the job

description. For each requirement, craft a statement that tells them: **a) where [company] you developed or used [x skill]; b) for how long [months and/or years]; and c) what you consider your [key successes] accomplishments to be around that skill.** Being able to state where you got the skill, how much depth of experience you have in it, and some positive results from it, will give the hiring manager exactly what they're looking for: your quantified and qualified experience. Rehearsing your answers on paper and out loud will move the information from short-term (one exposure) to long-term memory (minimum three exposures). This simple formula will help you answer the old "tell me about your experience" question. The formula will provide the necessary information, while keeping you from going off on a tangent. Remember: if you answer any given question with more than five to six sentences, you're in tangent territory.

4. **Now, research the organization.** Research its mandate [About Us], key stakeholders [Meet the Team], board members [About Us], client roster [Services], and company policies [Privacy Policy/ Human Resources Page/Mission Statement]. Also look at any press [public relations]—whatever's available on their website. Get to know this company! Your research should include any *recent* news releases (read: previous three months). You should be able to quote or paraphrase the company mandate from the website. Finally, check out any stakeholders' LinkedIn profiles. These will give you critical insight into what kind of people they are, what their credentials and/or education are, and what the company is doing (along

with *why* they're doing it). Informing yourself may also uncover some interests you have in common. *Remember that all shared experience and/or interests will help them relate to you more strongly.*

5. **Prepare three significant, concrete questions** regarding the role, company, team, culture, or key responsibilities of the job.

6. **Be prepared to discuss compensation**, although it's usually not recommended to discuss salary in a first-round interview, if you can help it. It's helpful to figure out in advance what salary "range" you seek. *Your range starts at what you need and tops out at what you want.* By offering a range, you're giving them a *signal* about where you want your salary to fall, while also giving them options. Options are good. I usually go with a $5K spread for entry-level jobs; a $5-10K spread for mid-management roles, and a $10-20K spread for senior management. (Refer to Chapter 17's "Negotiating Your Salary and Deal Points.")

> **""** *Never discuss salary in the first meeting. In my experience, the hiring time is the best time to get the biggest bump in salary. From there, you just get cost-of-living increases, unless you get another job. They'll ask you what you're making and I'd inflate it a bit. In order for it to work, the challenge you have is that it's a matter of what the company can actually afford.* **"**

—Jeffrey Elliott, chief executive officer
www.tablerockmedia.com

MINDSET ALERT! If you're invited to interview, congratulations, you're a *peer!* This means, that you're *not* a subordinate at that table. Everyone in that interview room brings a certain level of expertise—that's cool; they've earned it. But it doesn't make them *superior* to you. It just makes them *more experienced.* Get comfortable with that distinction! Recognize their expertise, but for heaven's sake, recognize your own, too, and ★ don't walk in there like a victim. Walk in like a pro! Instead of fearing or loathing interviews, why not view them as really cool opportunities to meet more of your industry peers and colleagues and get to know them? Different mindset, right? They may or may not hire you, now, or in the future. So do a good job, and set the stage for whatever future successes you might realize with a given team.

1. **Dress for success.** Google the company and check out any photo references that give you clues as to the *look* of the company. Google the executive profiles as well as the creative profiles. Get a sense of how people dress there. If in doubt, remember the old adage: "Dress for the job you want, not the job you have."

2. **Bring a fresh copy of your resume, as well as a list of three to five professional and/or peer references** listed cleanly on a separate sheet. Bringing references is a truly professional (read: facilitative) action to take. Please note that by law, employers cannot call your references without your permission. Offering your references upfront will help them save valuable time at a later date in the hiring process. Of course, don't neglect to alert your references to the fact that you're

applying for [role] with [company]. If you're not comfortable giving them your references up front, don't—check with your gut. Ideally (and alternatively) there will be recommendations and endorsements available for their review on your LinkedIn profile.

3. Allow yourself lots of travel time and **arrive five to ten minutes early**. Never arrive stressed out, panicky, or reactive to pressures from public transit, parking, or traffic. Ideally, if you haven't been to that location before, do a trial run a few days beforehand to ensure you know the area, where to park, and how to access the offices. Use your best manners with reception staff, where applicable.

4. **Prepare some "small talk,"** and have it at the ready for the first couple of minutes—as you're being guided to a meeting room. If you've done your research, you should be able to speak to some of the company's current successes, initiatives, etc. Connect on a *personal* level only if you have good reason to (like when you have a *professional interest* in common—you're at the interview to discuss business). Of course, if you are a Canadian, talking about the weather is fine, too, LOL! But why lose the opportunity to manage your messaging more tightly?

5. **Sit down, get comfortable; and ground your hands and feet** (i.e., don't swing around in your chair). Put your personal items *under* your chair and slip a fresh copy of your resume, your references, and (hopefully) a business card to the key stakeholder in the room. I like to put the documents down on the table in front of me and slide them across to the human resources

representative, if one is present. It's a professional courtesy to recognize HR's role in the process. Otherwise, just slide the documents over to the hiring manager.

6. The main focus of a first-round interview is to **defend your degree of match to the job's** skills (yet another reason why "crunching the job description" is a great idea). A secondary purpose of a first-round interview is to build a relationship/connection with *all* decision-makers (this includes your recruiter, if one is involved). ★ Note to self: don't ever minimize your recruiter's efforts/position.

7. Once the small talk is over, the hiring manager or HR rep will take over the process. Now we get into the nitty-gritty of the interview . . . and we "manage it." ★ Don't be shy to do your part to **keep the interview on track.** Be prepared to discuss three or four major responsibilities of the role. If you did the earlier exercise of rehearsing and/or writing up where [company] you acquired the [skill/knowledge area], how long [months or years] you employed the skill, and some key successes [accomplishments] in it, you are truly good to go!

8. **Maintain good eye contact**—travel from one person to the other, addressing each person, giving them all equal attention (but don't make like you're watching a Ping-Pong game).

9. **KILLER APP ALERT—Use First Names!** It's a really good practice to refer to panel participants (periodically*)*, using their first names. Addressing them thus

is a great way to personalize your message and build rapport. It also levels the playing field. ★ Don't *overuse* first names, but every now and again, you can respond with "Thanks, Mark, great question" or "To your point, Sheri..." It helps them relate to you. So, pepper the conversation with their first names when it feels natural. This is a nice *relational* way to build connection. Mirror their turns of phrase, as well as their body language, too, if you can. If someone "leans in" to you, lean in, as well. Show your interest in them as a potential teammate.

10. **During the course of the interview, you should be able to convey your business case** in four simple statements that tell hiring managers why you want this job. If you consider this a "to-die-for job," be sure to prepare your business case and deliver it. Let the hiring manager know you've put some thought into it. They'll see you as being motivated and committed (not to mention better prepared than any other candidate in front of them—score!) Further, job seekers should never be afraid to communicate their degree of interest in the position. ★ In fact, one of the greatest mistakes you can make is to *not* communicate your enthusiasm and interest in the role!

11. **Be prepared to (briefly) handle the salary discussion.** Remember, it's "purpose over pay" in a first-round interview. Salary negotiations are far better suited to second-round interviews (refer to Chapter 17's "Negotiating Your Salary and Deal Points"). But in brief, it rolls out like this: They say: "Can you tell us what compensation range you are expecting?" You respond with: "Can you please share with me the actual "range"

you've assigned to this role?" They will disclose something about the range. Digest that for a couple of seconds, and think about *where you would like to land in that range*. Then come back with: "Based on my [a], [b], [c] top skills/experience (offer them three main skills or knowledge areas you have that relate most directly to the job), I feel it would be appropriate to come in at the bottom, middle, *or* top-end of the range (choose one)." You're not talking about actual dollars here; you are just *signalling* where you want the dollars to come in. You are simply indicating where you want to go with the negotiations and *giving them options within their stated range*. And then take charge and redirect the conversation back to the role at hand.

12. **Interview Wrap-Up:** Thank you(s). As you leave, address each person by name. "Mark, it was a pleasure to meet you." "Sheri, thanks for your valuable time." Host it. Facilitate it. "It's been great to meet you all," with your hand outstretched for a nice, solid handshake. Maintain good eye contact and don't forget to smile! **Don't hesitate to ask about next steps** as you are leaving—this serves as good *small talk* on the way out. Maybe: "Can you share the hiring process with me, going forward?" This will keep you from going home and chewing off your own leg with anxiety about next steps. Assure them of your availability by cell/email should they have additional questions.

13. **After the interview:** Be available, and stay available! Make sure if they do end up in your voice mail (★ bad form alert!) that your voice-mail message or email auto-response has a warm message, with full name

and proposed response time. True professionals make a point of always setting others up for success! ★ Conversely, never take a phone call if you don't have the time, or aren't able to give the caller your full attention (that's bad form, too!)

The goal of the first-round interview is to make them want to hire you. Usually, if they want you (and only you) they'll make it work financially. That's why you keep reminding them of your skills, best attributes, *and* business case . . . *before* you signal where you want to go money-wise.

WHAT NOT TO DO IN A FIRST-ROUND INTERVIEW . . .

★ Don't answer questions by throwing everything in but the kitchen sink. When answering a question, if you've gone beyond five or six sentences, you're starting to wander. Again, this is where rehearsing your skills statements comes in *really* handy! If you do find yourself wandering, stop yourself, reiterate and/or reference the actual question, and recap your top three points regarding the skill or knowledge area concerned (e.g., where you did it, how long, and how well).

> **"** *Learn how to interview, and be concise with your answers. Be specific and ask for what you want.* **"**
>
> —Kadon Douglas, communications & engagement manager
> **www.wift.com**

★ **Don't over-share.** You're aware there is such a thing as "too much information", right? Impulse control is a highly valued life skill. Learn when and where to draw the line. You want to be professional and poised. You want to display appropriate, healthy boundaries.

★ **Don't get personal.** The only level of personal you can go to, is perhaps mentioning that you noticed in your research that they like [x] hobby, [y] group, or [z] interest. It's got to be public knowledge—meaning: You shouldn't ask if they have kids or a partner or anything about their work histories.

★ **Don't go overboard on emotions**. It's OK to emote, of course. Just don't overdo it. Look on the interview as more opportunities to build impulse control skills.

★ **Watch your body language.** If you don't know about body language yet, you need to. Look it up and study it a bit (like, for the rest of your life, LOL!). Body language is incredibly important. Aggressive, avoidant, hedgy, curt, and making statements v. asking questions are all, literally, "positions" that you don't want to be in. Open-ness, "leaning-in," smiling, using some broad hand gestures (not overly emphatic), asking questions v. making statements, and sporadically using first names, read as more inclusive behaviours. Inclusion or exclusion? You decide.

★ **LANDMINE ALERT! Don't let the interviewer "derail the interview" into small talk about "who you know in the industry."** This is a landmine that could tip them into *backdoor-referencing* you with a person you both mutually know. Backdoor referencing is relatively widespread, not to mention *extremely uncool* (and if I'm not mistaken, in most jurisdictions, actually illegal). The reason you don't want to talk about "who you know" is really quite important: You may have friends or colleagues in common. When they know someone you know, they sometimes call those people to make informal inquiries about you. So don't volunteer any names of friends or colleagues, unless you are 100% certain that your working relationships (past and present) with those people are intact, and that they would be truly prepared to represent your greatest strengths. I repeat: *intact and fully prepared to represent you in the most positive way.* The closer the hiring manager is to a "backdoor reference" the more information they'll be able to get on you—good, bad, or otherwise.

> **"** *There's no shortage of career-sabotaging mistakes a person can make, but gaining a reputation for being difficult to work with, and being a disruptive and negative presence in the workplace will quickly overtake whatever skill and talent you bring to the job.* **"**

—Hudson Mack, veteran news director and anchor
www.harbourpublishing.com/title/HudsonMack

★ There is a **recent trend afoot** in the labour markets, where some Gen Z/iGen job seekers are **"no-showing" on interviews**. Worse, they don't even call to advise that they won't be attending—they just don't show up. Do not be this person! My memory as a recruiter is long and fast when it comes to unprofessional behaviours. You have a long career ahead of you in your industry—so don't.burn.bridges! Hiring managers will remember your name if you're a no-show. You will be remembered for being unprofessional and disrespecting others' valuable time. You may grow up later on the subject, but by then, it'll be too late. You will have left an indelible negative first impression that will throw shade on your entire career.

After the interview, go home and resuscitate your job search. That's right: Go straight back into job-search research. It will help occupy your mind while a given hiring process rolls out. It will also ensure you aren't placing all your eggs in one basket. Invariably, the hiring process takes longer than any candidate can tolerate. Two days is only two days. It's a nightmare for you while you wait, but to them it's only two days. It could be a minimum of a week or two, sometimes three, before you even hear from them again. So refocus on your job search. Let the process play out.

Remember: a deal is not a deal until it's a deal.

HOW TO BULLETPROOF A SECOND-ROUND INTERVIEW

1. **A second-round interview is all about "cultural fit."**
   You are likely to be invited to meet additional company stakeholders that relate to your area of responsibility, and they will definitely have to give you a thumbs-up before the hiring manager decides on your hire. You will want to make an effort to connect with and relate to, *each* stakeholder, and pay attention to their individual concerns. If they are participating in the interview, they definitely have a "stake" in the hire. So you want to listen to them, paraphrase their concerns where you can, use their first names, and generally "woo them" into your camp by being prepared, professional and poised, and by addressing their individual concerns (and you will, if you've *actively listened*.)

2. **Please know that companies are seeking a return on their investment**—you need to be sure you communicate not only that you *can* do the job, but you *will* do the job! Hiring managers need to hear this from you. New hires are seriously expensive for companies—they can't afford to on-board you for a few short months before you move onto something more exciting. They want and expect you to stay for a reasonable amount of time. The safest guesstimate on that time-frame is two to five years—long enough for you to develop deeper expertise in a given role, and to make it worth their while to hire you in the first place.

3. **At this point, they like you, and are seriously interested in you.** Hopefully, you are feeling warm and fuzzy too. On the negative side of things, the second-round interview is an opportunity for decision-makers to review any deficiencies or concerns they may have with respect to your skills, experience and/or knowledge. On the positive side, they are looking for *you* to affirm your *capacity* to do the job, your *willingness* to do the job, your *ability to fit in*, and your *staying power* in the job. Be this person. Wow them on all fronts. Give them what they want!

4. **The second-round interview is the time to pull out any remaining questions that you need clarification on.** These could be about the job, the team, the company, your boss, performance expectations, and deal points like vacation/time off, etc. (Refer to Chapter 17's "Negotiating Your Salary and Deal Points.")

5. **If they make you an offer,** it is perfectly appropriate to ask for twenty-four to forty-eight hours to review it with

your lawyer, life partner, etc. **If they don't make an offer** despite things seeming to have gone well, just go with the flow. Be warm, personable, ask about next steps, and make a gracious exit.

6. Send a **thank-you note** once again, this time a little less formal and a little more social in nature. Good manners never get old. Reiterate your *short-format business case/expression of interest,* and be clear that you are excited about the job.

WHAT NOT TO DO IN A SECOND-ROUND INTERVIEW . . .

★ **Don't show your full hand** financially until you know they really want you—i.e., a second-round interview. If they are seriously talking money, they probably want you. So now it is up to you to negotiate a win-win. (Refer to Chapter 17's "Negotiating Your Salary and Deal Points.")

★ **Never, ever, *ever* attend a second-round interview unless you truly want the job,** and are ready to commit to the company.

★ **Don't let your guard down by getting too comfortable.** Continue playing by the rules. This is business. Keep it right there!

★ **Be careful not to verbalize any *assumptions* about the company**. They will tell you far faster than you can tell them. Ask . . . don't tell.

★ **Refrain from asking any details about your competition or how many people are trying for the role**—that just puts a spotlight on your insecurity. It may also signal them that you are more concerned with your own success than the company's success. Your skills, knowledge, and demonstrated track record are what's important, and are the best points to emphasize.

MINDSET ALERT—You are not alone! Please note it is not unheard of for decision-makers to have two final candidates when it comes down to the wire, right up to and including the referencing stage. The hire can always go sideways, and if it does, they want to have a "Plan B" lined up. Makes sense! So just play by the rules, keep your head on straight, and provide them with any/everything they need. If it's meant to be, it will be. If it doesn't work out, it is usually for the right reasons—some of which you may get to know, some of which you may never know. Stay humble. And be cool. Keep playing by the rules.

INTERVIEW QUESTIONS YOU WILL WANT TO PREPARE FOR . . .

"What's your greatest weakness/strength?" This is a question you should be prepared to answer at any given time in your career. An easy trick to use, is to go back mentally through your work history, and recall a time when you got into some hot water on the job (for whatever reason) and tell them about it. The reason you go into the past, is that it helps you avoid discussing any recent issues. The trick is to *own* the fact that you are not perfect but that you are open to growing and learning. Tell them what you learned from it.

Another way to frame strengths and weaknesses: Weaknesses can be strengths, and strengths can be weaknesses. Personally, I could mention my (intensely) high work ethic, but would also state that it can be a weakness if I don't keep it in check, and others can't meet my expectations. Basically, they are looking for self-awareness in this question. Own your flaws, and show them that you are the type of person who learns from them. Self-awareness is a true strength and a highly valued soft skill.

If any question from a hiring manager starts with: "Tell me about a time when . . . " you are being asked a "behavioural" question. They are looking to see how you would react, or have reacted, to a challenging situation. It could be asking anything from how you handled a tricky intra-personal work relationship, to how you "crisis-managed" a client situation that went sideways. They are looking for examples in your past on how you faced (and conquered) a difficult situation. So go into your past work experience and *offer them an example of a successful resolution to a workplace issue*. It's smart to think about this question in advance, and have some prepared answers for how well you handle situational challenges.

What to Do When Asked if You Would "Work for Free"

LANDMINE ALERT! Sometimes, you are asked to work for free, and you will need to carefully assess the pros and cons. It all comes down to figuring out what the opportunity is worth to you. BTW, in case no one has ever told you, you can always just.say.no. Graciously, but no.

Reasons for working for free might include a) to get your foot in the door and gain exposure to an experience, skills, or a community that will add value to your portfolio and extend your social equity; b) a key success in this area would be a great resume-builder/marketing tool; c) volunteering for and/or gaining experience in an important cause—again, that lends additional value to your growing portfolio; and/or d) the opportunity to explore or network in a sector you would like to work in.

Factors for not paying you can include: a) the company doesn't have steady financing yet, so they offer you something on barter, like brand reach, or a certain type of exposure that would benefit you; b) it's a start-up company, so you only get paid if the venture is successful and/or they offer you stock options; c) it's an "in-demand gig" that others are willing to volunteer for; or d) because your relationship is personal, and "you're friends."

If you do choose to work for free: a) make sure the timeline on any given assignment has a "hard" end date; b) make sure that you get something out of it, like a website testimonial, a LinkedIn recommendation, a hotlink to a page where your work might be showcased, credit on the project, written recognition of your contribution in a news release, or introductions to key stakeholders in the community; more critically c) ask for serious consideration for the next paying gig; and d) *get that serious consideration in writing!* It could be as simple as an email from you to the partners, confirming any parameters or terms of reference that were discussed. ★ You will only have to learn the hard lesson once, if you don't "paper it". Set yourself up for success initially, and be sure to document your successes on the job—in writing.

How to Answer: "Do You Have Any Questions for Us?"—aka Good Questions to Ask in an Interview . . .

This is your opportunity to ask questions about the job, your boss, the team, the company, the culture, performance expectations, the compensation and benefits, work "tools" (computer, iPhone, etc.), expected hours of work, flex time, media policies, expense budgets, parking, work/life balance, professional-development opportunities, and their office policy on bringing your dog to work. Did I miss anything?

What can you tell me about the culture of the company? You need to find out about the internal culture *before* you take on a permanent role there. Asking about their culture is a great way for you to signal that you want to fit in, and that you are planning for it. Check whether their values resonate with you, and whether their company policies suit your professional wants and needs.

LANDMINE ALERT! Consider it a heads up if certain **stakeholders don't see eye to eye about the company direction or culture**. If they are at loggerheads with each other over any given issue, that could be a real set-up for failure for you.

What can you tell me about the team? You really want to gather as much information about your prospective teammates as possible. How big is the team? What aspects of their performance and/or culture serve the company best? What are their strengths, and weaknesses? Particular successes? Do they participate regularly in cultural or community activities? Can you buy-into these activities?

What are the best steps I can take to prepare for this role and enhance my ability to hit the ground running? They will *love* this question—it tells them that you are thinking on your feet, and that you hold their interests front and centre (i.e., before your own).

What can I do in my first three months, and my first twelve months, to make this hire a resounding success for you? Asking about quarterly and annual goals for the position is key to setting yourself up for success. Once the key performance indicators (KPIs) are established, you can e-mail a summary of them to your direct report after you're hired. Having your KPIs established up front and in writing is a great insurance policy for not going wrong on the job. Then, of course, note the KPIs in your calendar and deliver on them! (Refer to Chapter 18's "How to Start Your New Job on the Right Foot").

Does the company offer any professional-development incentives? It's fine to ask if they will support your professional growth by contributing fees for a trade-association membership, paying for you to attend conferences related to your role, and/or offering ongoing skills training as applicable. The ultimate win-win is when a company is prepared to commit to you in the same way they expect you to commit to them. Way to go in the life-long learning department! If you get professional development built into your deal, consider it a total score! You'll be able to further extend your individual brand and your knowledge, and build *vital* contacts for the future.

Does the company offer health benefits, bonuses, or RRSP programs? Memorize this question. Don't minimize it, by only asking about health benefits. Learn to deliver the question like a stream of consciousness. Even if they don't offer bonuses or RRSP programs, it doesn't hurt to ask. You are not breaking any rules. You will be darned sorry later if you find out that they do indeed offer bonuses, but neglected to include them in your particular deal simply because you didn't ask. I've seen it happen more than once.

What is your policy for cost-of-living increases? This question is about when you will see your next raise, and it can be a daunting one to tackle. Get used to having this discussion and making this ask as early as possible in your career. Many companies hire you at a certain salary, and then you have to fight tooth and nail for any increases going forward. Find out if performance reviews are held on an annual basis. *Is the performance review process formalized, based on merit, and consistently rewarded?* ★ If they shy away from this, you need to think long and hard about whether you want to join this company. Do you want to give them two to five years of your life without any chance of increasing your pay or marginally moving up the ranks? Is it worth it to you to take the job on, knowing that over time, you will not be able to gain any measurable ground in terms of debt reduction or overall life-savings? If you're not happy with this from day one, imagine how you're going to feel at year two or three! It's largely untenable. Honour any negative feelings or doubts you might have here.

> " *Continuous curiosity: I've made a few interesting jumps that were driven by a willingness to be curious, and open to opportunities. Future-proofing is attitudinal. You want talent with bigger perspectives in sociology, human behaviour, psychology, politics, and policy. Focus more on macro skills than micro skills.* "

—Mark Prasuhn, president
www.cmucollege.com

Thank-you notes are critically important. They show good manners, for sure, but more importantly, they give you an opportunity to reiterate a mini-version of your business case (you know, all together now: "Why you, why now, why this role, why this company"?). The email should be sent at nine a.m. (on the nose!) the next business day—you want to be first in their mailbox. You can also always use a thank-you note to ask an important question that you might have missed, but only if it is mission critical, and something for which you absolutely need clarification. A better idea after you reiterate your mini-business case, is to ask them if there is anything you can provide them to make the hiring decision a little easier (in case any one stakeholder is sitting on the fence). Be straightforward, be enthusiastic, and keep the note short and relatively "social" and "warm." Continue to add full contact information.

★ **It is never a good idea to ask for "feedback" on an interview.** Hiring managers are generally too busy for stuff like this, and really don't have time to "take care of you." *It is your job to take care of you.* Further, the question sets decision-makers up for failure because they have to make an effort to "appease you"—and they have to be super careful about what they share with you from a legal perspective. Finally, one is never really prepared to respond to negative feedback, and as a result, generally does a bad job of it. Or, worse, gets defensive! That is even more uncomfortable. So, just let it rest. Listen to what your gut tells you about the experience. If you think you did something wrong, you probably did. Trust your instincts, and learn from it by using the experience to up your game next time.

What happens if you messed something up in a big way during the interview, and it's the job of your dreams? Send them a brief email that will help clarify your issue and your perspective by offering them greater context. Keep it short and humble. Honesty is always the best policy. See what happens. It doesn't hurt to try; it only hurts *not* to try.

> " *I would ask more people to take a chance on me. I took chances on myself and they paid off, but I believe I would be farther ahead now if I had aligned myself more closely with some of the amazing people I've met in my career. I would find more mentors, and apply for more freelancing jobs. I would find ways to work faster and harder and bolder at the beginning of my career, to build the momentum, reputation, and foundation for a long-lasting career.* "

—Chanda Chevannes, filmmaker, writer, educator
  www.chandachevannes.com

CHAPTER 17

NEGOTIATING YOUR SALARY AND DEAL POINTS

They ask: "What are your expectations in terms of salary?"

MIC DROP! Eighty percent of job seekers cannot answer this question with confidence.

Savvy negotiating skills are essential to ensuring you get the compensation package you want and deserve. It follows that you get better at it, as you move through your career. Super-pros will start developing negotiating skills as early as possible in their career, as they recognize that they will need those skills for the rest of their working lives.

So let's get some perspective by breaking the negotiating process into three easy stages:

1. First, you *"prepare for the discussion"*;

2. Then you *"have the discussion"*; and

3. Finally, you *"close the deal,"* achieving the desired win-win for both parties.

STAGE 1: HOW TO PREPARE FOR "THE SALARY AND DEAL DISCUSSION"

When you apply for a job, one of your main concerns will be your compensation. And that's fine. But . . . please understand that the employer's main concerns are more focused on how you will add value to the company and how you will contribute to its bottom line. Only after the employer is satisfied that your skills and knowledge will be of value over any other candidates', will they explore discussing an offer.

How well you handle compensation discussions, cannot only have a serious impact on your baseline salary, but it can actually be the deciding factor in whether you get the position! Think of it like this: If you cannot manage negotiating your salary, how are you going to be negotiating on behalf of the company, going forward? It's well worth developing negotiating skills!

1.1 GET COMFORTABLE WITH THE CONCEPT OF "FAIR MARKET VALUE"

What exactly is "fair market value"? Let's say you need to hire a service person or contractor to do some work for you. A copywriter? Graphic artist? Webmaster? Dog walker? For any specialty area, you will make an automatic assumption about what you might have to pay for those services. You would consider the range/rate that you think a contractor might ask for hourly, and the number of hours it would likely take them to deliver on the job. If it's a big job, you will want to think in terms of weekly, monthly, or annual rates; if it's a smaller job, you'll want to think hourly, daily, or weekly rates. The onus is on you to figure each of these out and, over time, be prepared to state hard ranges.

As an example, let's say I want to hire a gardener to do an afternoon's work on my property. So I go through the mental exercise: I bet it would cost me anywhere from (lowball—a basic garden clean-up kind of person) $25 per hour, or $100 total, to (highball—garden planning and design) $50 per hour, or $200 total, for work roughly equalling four hours. (Four hours is generally considered a typical "minimum call-out" in most industries.) So, **fair market value is the "range" that you think it is going to roughly cost for the time spent at a given job**—in this case, $100-$200 dollars for a landscaper's afternoon's work. Seems fair, right?

The same applies to the salary for any job. Give some thought to the *range* you think would apply for [x years' experience] in [y area/sector/skill]. If you have serious doubts about your answer, then your instincts are telling you that you are off the mark—listen to them! However, if you *think* the job range is likely to pay from [x-y] figure and the thought *feels* right, then you probably *are* right. So, trust yourself, and go with it. *If you have any residual doubts, adjust your ranges until you arrive at a comfortable answer for you.*

Ask yourself what the salary range is, that you are seeking. Having a *range* means you have options, and by offering a range, you give an employer options. Your range should *start with what you need to live on* (lowball), and *end with what you want* (best-case scenario/ highball—without going over the top). I suggest a range that gives them a good spread so that both parties have options to work within.

Of course, if you have tremendous difficulty with this, you could always ask a senior-management person or executive for their thoughts on the subject. **Test out your range on some "business people" you know,** and see what they think it should be, considering the role and your level of experience in it. ★ But please: professionals only! Don't ask your friends or peers—they usually don't know what to ask for, any more than you do.

> **❝** *Sometimes, you might be paid less than fair market value, vis-à-vis your responsibilities and your role. It's the balance between the pay and the other factors . . . Like, maybe you'll have more opportunities to learn and develop your career path, or greater opportunities for advancement, or a better title. You may be working longer hours, but your job satisfaction makes it all worth it. You may love the business, or share a vision with the CEO—all of these can outweigh any potential monetary loss. It's the balance that's important. To me, it's not as simple as negotiating an extra $5K—it's all of these things combined together.* **❞**

—Jeffrey Elliott, chief executive officer
www.tablerockmedia.com

You want to be prepared for the salary discussion. Flying by the seat of your pants is not only regretable, it's completely unnecessary, messy, and just doesn't do you any service. Plus, it signals your recruiter/hiring manager that you don't know how to negotiate (yet). Not a good sign.

1.2 GET SOME PERSPECTIVE ON NEGOTIATING

Please make an effort to **get the negotiating process in perspective:** It is a negotiation—not a conspiracy. This is no time to play cloak-and-dagger games. Be prepared, honest, and forthcoming—and stay flexible.

Hiring managers expect to negotiate with you, and expect you to be equally prepared to negotiate with them.

Style awareness: Be aware of your personal style. Are you timid? Assertive? Defensive? Avoidant? Get some honest 360 feedback on your style, and learn to hit the middle ground in terms of "tone." Rehearse out loud how you would discuss the salary negotiation—it's *so* worth it!

Be able to **articulate your skills sets, as well as your knowledge areas**—e.g., you are skilled in the craft of television production, but you also understand the "business of television." Skills and knowledge are two separate things.

Do your research on the company you're negotiating with: How healthy are they financially? Are they cash-strapped or fairly profitable? Says who?

Understand it's a negotiation just like any other—you are seeking the middle ground, not absolutes.

★ **Don't play "mind games"** with yourself, like: "They're probably going to give the job to someone who will take less" (you don't *know* that). Or "I'm afraid I'll ask too low." Or "I'm worried about my ask being too high." Or, the classic: "I can make more money as a freelancer." Maybe! You may make more money over the short term as a freelancer, but you may also suffer disruptive periods of unemployment as well. Whereas slow and steady full-time employment will likely provide opportunities for better money management over the longer term, plus benefits, plus pension and/or potential stock options. It's a trade off, and only you can decide which is better for you, and why. This being said, think through your range, stay there, and don't second-guess yourself. This is no time to hedge your bets or push your luck. In my opinion, if an employer wants you badly enough (if you've done a good job handling the recruiting process and your skills match the role), they will ante up (some!). Trust me.

★ **Remove all "personal" attachments to the process**—You make your ask—and you either get it or you don't. ★ Whatever you do, don't make it personal, or take it personally. Be the true professional you know that you are, and just stick to business.

1.3 ESTABLISH YOUR BASELINE SALARY OBJECTIVES

Know the difference between what you need and what you want, and spread it out over a range that co-relates to your years of experience.

Be able to state your salary expectations comfortably in differing formats: daily, weekly, monthly, and annually.

I use this as a **handy rule of thumb for "salary ranges":** 1-5 years: $5K range spread; 5-10 years: $6-8K range spread; 10-15 years: $8-12K range spread; and 15-20 years: $12-15-20K range spread. Again, this always depends on the depth of skills and knowledge you bring to the role vis-à-vis what they are asking for.

1.4 CONSULTING FEES

Be able and ready to state your fees in hourly, daily, weekly, monthly, and annual ranges. Know your ask inside out. What's your day rate? What feels right to you for eight hours of work? What do you think you should be earning in a weekly rate, as a freelancer? *Remember, your rates range from what you need to what you want.* Be realistic and authentic. Get some figures down on paper for yourself. Will you accept $15-20 an hour, or do you want $40-50? Or, do you expect $100-120 an hour based on your subject matter expertise? You can always gauge your fees according to your last job, increase the salary a little, and then break it down into the above categories. You need to work these figures through roughly, with yourself, so that you can offer some kind of answer when someone asks you what your salary expectations (or rates) are. And you have to start somewhere—so start! If you're out of line, you will soon discover it and you will learn from it for next time and adjust accordingly. Everyone needs to learn to do this.

Note: For freelancers/consultants, it is always helpful (and usually a lot easier) to just ask a client what their budget actually is, for a given gig. They will have done the math—believe me. And they will be grateful for the opportunity to speak honestly with you about costs/fees, and any limitations they may have. ★ But don't let this be an excuse not to have the above breakdowns at the ready.

1.5 RESEARCH & REHEARSE

Research the company ahead of time—connect with any company employees you can find online. If you handle your introduction well, you may open the door to asking about the company's compensation best practices and parameters. Another, perhaps even better tactic, is to look up *former* staff and, after establishing a bit of a relationship, ask for some guidance around salary ranges at that company. Again, it's critical to learn how to ask the hard questions. Politely. Appropriately. But be sure to ask. The more you learn to flex this muscle, the greater your overall life gains will be. Think about that! And as always, offer your connection something in return that is valuable to them, or will be valuable to them, down the road.

Research similar roles in your industry by talking to friends and/or colleagues. ★ Don't take their *advice*, but do take their *facts*, and thank them for them. And be sure to pay it forward for others later.

Rehearse in real time—out loud—*what* you're going to say and *how* you're going to say it. Rehearsal is the difference between hitting the nail on the head and not hitting it at all. Rehearsing your points *out loud, stem to stern, multiple times,* moves simple thoughts circling around your short-term memory, to permanent facts lodged in your long-term memory. Your brain will never let you down. So set it up for success already.

KILLER APP ALERT—Rehearse! When people rehearse something, whether it's a presentation or a script for a phone call, they eventually get to a point where they make a mistake, do a hard stop—and then go back and start rehearsing again from the beginning. Don't be this person! When you're rehearsing, teach yourself to burn through the entire script, whether you make mistakes or not, each and every time. If you stop and begin at the top again whenever you make a mistake, you tend to get really good at the front end of your presentation, but not so great on the bottom end. So . . . full rehearsals/run-throughs are us!

STAGE 2—HOW TO HAVE THE "SALARY AND DEAL DISCUSSION"

2.1 THE MONEY CONVERSATION - ROUND ONE

They ask you: "What salary are you looking for?"

You answer: "Can you share with me the *range* you've assigned to this role?" And then be quiet, and wait it out. Don't be afraid of silence. Everyone hates silence, and will do damned near anything to fill the void. ★ This is where inexperienced, unprepared job seekers start to back pedal and try to justify his/her ask. Don't be this person. Give them time to respond, and offer up their assigned range.

If they are slow to respond, you might nudge them a little by stating, "I am sure you have a range in mind for/assigned to this role." And then be quiet again. Wait it out.

They (have to) respond: $[x-y]K, or, $50-60K, or, $80-100K, or, whatever. Sometimes, they refuse to disclose their range, and try to fob you off. That's ok too. In this case, I usually recommend making a joke, to break the ice and the tension. So I'll kindly say: "I bet your range is somewhere between $10K and $150K annually. Am I right?" If you deliver it authentically, they usually appreciate the nudge as well as the humour, and anti-up some kind of response.

When they do respond, you need to come back with a direct (hopefully positive) statement, like: "That seems in line with what I was thinking." Or: "That is a little lower than I was anticipating, but I'm sure we can work with something close to this range." Whatever you sense, you need to tell them your honest opinion. If it is too low (and you still want the job), you can always ask for additional perks—once you both agree on a baseline range. Establishing the baseline range will be your biggest hurdle.

Once they have stated their range, you then carry on the discussion by making strong statements about your top skills for the job: "Given my [a], [b], and [c] skills and/or [x], [y], and [z] knowledge and experience, I believe it would be appropriate to come in at (choose one) the *low*, *mid,* or *high en*d of the range." So you are *signalling them* where you want to go with the negotiation without actually disclosing a hard figure—all the while reinforcing your ask with your business case. Whew! Good work!

MINDSET ALERT: What you are doing here, is simply telling the company *why you're the right person and why they should hire you*, instead of leaving them to "do the math". Own your skills, your knowledge, and your place (status) in your professional community. Manage your message (i.e., ★ don't leave it to them to figure out if you are the right person for the job—tell them!).

★ Please know that stating a hard, single figure locks you in, and only serves to narrow your options . . . and theirs. So hit them with a range. It's just safer.

Once you've signalled to them where you want the dollars to land, take charge of the situation and re-direct the conversation back to the job—get in and get out of the money conversation, fast. Let them know what you're thinking money-wise, then, pivot straight back to *purpose over pay,* and the requirements of the job.

2.2 THE MONEY CONVERSATION - ROUND TWO

The money conversation comes up again in a second-round interview—things are getting serious, and it's normal for employers to want to clarify details around compensation. They will intro the conversation with something akin to "You let us know in our last discussion that you were looking for $60-70K." Or whatever.

You respond with another positive statement about your excitement about the role, and then repeat: "Given my skills [name them] and/or knowledge/experience [name them], I believe it would be appropriate to come in between $[x-y]K." Note: Here, you are offering a tighter $[x-y]K spread within the range previously expressed. Stay quiet. Now, you have let them know what your thinking is, and they have let you know what their thoughts are. If it's only a $5K difference and you're the preferred candidate, they usually try to find a way to make it work.

But then again, they might go one more round . . .

"We were really hoping for $[lower figure]K." You come back with: "Let's settle in the middle: $[offer middle figure]K and we have a deal." Boom! Win-win!

Then, based on how satisfied everyone is feeling thus far, and if the timing is right, you might ask about additional deal points (refer to next page, item 2.4).

MINDSET ALERT! As you plan and rehearse negotiating, try to see yourself as a product or service—and think about ways to "introduce" "promote" or "sell" that product/service to the company. **De-personalize the situation** and look at it strictly in business terms. You provide a product, service, or experiential knowledge that relates directly to their business imperative and needs. Keep it right there. It's not about you. It's about your *skills, knowledge,* and *experience.*

Negotiating an appropriate compensation package is not a game, a conspiracy, a competition, or a test. **Negotiating a straightforward business process/exchange in which you discuss deal points**. The intention is to arrive at a fair and even-handed negotiation, with which both employer and future employee are comfortable, and in which both parties' expectations and needs are met.

The employer's aim is to attain your services at the lowest possible price-point. Your aim is to get the best possible compensation package for your services. Stick to your predetermined minimum and maximum salary range; there are other jobs that will meet your needs if this one does not.

2.4 ADDITIONAL NEGOTIABLE DEAL POINTS

- Start date

- Annual cost-of-living raise

- Health benefits (you *can* ask to waive the three-month probation period)

- Technology/work tools

- Holiday time/comp time/flex time

- Work-life balance

- Cloud computing

- Professional development: seminars/webinars, workshops, memberships, conferences, and educational programs, alumni groups, support for grant scholarships or fellowships

- Bonuses: signing bonus, profitability bonus, stock/equity bonuses, performance-based bonus

- RRSP contributions

- Car allowance

- Termination clause: Most people accept the "one-week's salary-per year model." But if you're really worth it, and you know it, how about asking for more? A week-and-a-half's salary per year? Or two weeks' salary per year, for senior-level roles? What do you have to lose by asking? You only lose if you don't ask. The more senior you are, the more likely the termination clause can grow in your favour. Research termination clauses and information yourself *before* you're in the position of trying to negotiate one.

Consider the above "additional negotiating deal points" as a shopping list, being mindful that you can't ask for all of it. Pick two, three, or four items that you feel would be the most beneficial to you at this stage of your career, and gently *inquire* about them during the first- *and* second-round interviews. Split your asks up over the two interviews. That way, when it comes to settling your deal, four items won't come as a surprise. They will probably give you half of what you want . . . so choose wisely. Get the biggest bang for your buck that you can, at this particular hiring stage. Think long term: Which of these perks is going to best set you up for future success?

Subject Matter Expertise (SME): It is known that it takes 10K hours to develop subject-matter expertise in any given area. The more senior you are and the more "star power" you have, the more you can ask for. At the entry level, you don't have a lot of power or options. As you grow your expertise and your personal brand in your area of expertise, however, you can increase your ask.

The best time to negotiate is when you get hired. Certainly not *after* you get hired. Once you're hired, your negotiating power for subsequent raises drops dramatically—they will probably agree to annual cost-of-living increases, but not much more. If, however, they are *promoting you*, then you have an opportunity to increase your ask(s) once again.

> **" "** *You have to know your worth. I've gotten to the point in my career where I pretty much know what I want. But I didn't always feel this way. Back in my twenties, they'd offer a salary, and I'd say thank you very much! I was grateful for whatever they would send my way. Through the years, I've learned a lot: I have a sense of what salary I want now, what's competitive, what I need to make it worth my while. I have a much better sense now of what the market will pay. When you're younger, stay flexible. When you're older, you can be much more selective. That only comes with experience.* **"**

—Alisyn Camerota, CNN anchor
www.alisyncamerota.com
www.cnn.com/shows/new-day

STAGE 3—CLOSING THE DEAL!

3.1 REVIEW AND FINALIZE THE CONTRACT

Human resources/hiring managers understand that you have employment needs, so **be sure to communicate your employment needs**! Let HR and hiring managers guide you through the process. That's what they are there for. Again, they *expect* to negotiate with you, and they will truly appreciate knowing what your concerns are, so that they can address them. Take the opportunity to clarify exactly what you need with HR, in order to be a long-term success in the job. Let's say you need every second Friday afternoon off for childcare, or you've already booked a vacation two months from now. You can plan around these things: Delay the start date, be available on a limited basis while you're away, compute from the road, etc. It's preferable if you're honest and just communicate your needs.

It's OK to have HR department generate a second-draft contract that incorporates any adjustments you wish to make. So take this opportunity to clarify what you need in order to be a long-term success in the job.

It's also OK to take a couple of days or a weekend to review and sign off on an employment contract. ★ **Don't shy away from getting professional advice**: review the offer with an employment lawyer. If you don't get professional advice, you'll be sorry you didn't. Let the HR manager know your timing ("I want to review it with my partner, who's away until Friday. How about we finalize Monday afternoon?"). Then, stick to your commitment to finalize that day.

KILLER APP ALERT—Create an Entry Strategy! Discuss creating an "entry strategy" (also known as the "cover-your-butt clause") with your hiring manager. An entry strategy addresses the employer's performance expectations in a) the first three months; and b) the first twelve months. When they make clear statements about their expectations of your performance in the first three and twelve months in the role, confirm those facts by email with your direct report when you begin your position. Then, make those expectations top priorities in your job—and deliver on them. Twelve months from now, they will have no recourse but to admit you have earned your next raise and/or bonus, if you provide proof of having delivered on your joint mandate. (Refer to Chapter 18's "How to Start Your New Job on the Right Foot")

" *My personal advice that I wish I'd learned much earlier in my career is to run everything through an employment lawyer. It's worth the cost! The termination (exit) clause is going to be based on what they are legally mandated to do—you need to follow the letter of the law. Work with your lawyer. The best results are predetermined beforehand, when you sign your deal. Building a termination clause is a good learning experience!*

—Jeffrey Elliott, chief executive officer
www.tablerockmedia.com

3.2 EXIT & ENTRY "POSITIONING STATEMENTS"

Create an "exit positioning statement" before you leave your current role—actually, develop it *before* you hand in your notice. Develop a *similar/*concomitant "entry positioning statement" that you share with all your friends and colleagues, as you begin your new role.

Creating an "exit positioning statement" is critical. Plan exactly what you want to say to your employer about why you are moving on, as well as your *rationale* for making the move, vis-à-vis your career. Be sure to say something nice and/or gracious about them, like: "I learned a great deal here" or, "I'd never have been able to secure this new role without the support and business guidance I received from this team"—whatever. Those are my words, not yours. But do have something positive to say. Say it, and keep saying it. Display a positive outlook going forward, and stay professional and courteous. Lean heavily on telling people that this is part of your career plan. Manage your message at all times (★ or others will manage it for you). You are in charge of your message, so be in charge!

Create a similar statement that you can use as an "entry positioning statement" that you share publicly when you are starting a new role. It's an important part of personal brand management. Your business case—why you, why now, why this role, and why this company—comes in real handy here (again)!

★ Don't wait for others to figure out, make assumptions, or draw independent (and usually inaccurate) conclusions about your career moves. *You* tell *them*! Create your *exit* positioning statement for the old company and your *entry* positioning statement for the new company. Tell it to your friends and colleagues. Make the same statements to your mother and your cat. Once again, stick to your exit and entry statements like glue.

3.3 WHAT IF THE POSITION IS NOT WHAT YOU ARE LOOKING FOR, AFTER ALL?

Sometimes you discover through the interview process that the role is actually not what you're looking for, and that **you need to extricate yourself from the hiring process,** while keeping the door open with the company for future opportunities. This can happen! You get cold feet, or you were uneasy at first, and now you're *real uneasy* about taking the job. The clear answer in this case is: don't! Another one will come up. **Explain to the hiring manager what your concerns are—** whether you feel under- or over-qualified, or that the pay scale is too low to keep you in the lifestyle you are accustomed to, or that the timing isn't right, or you are unsure about the fit with team . . . Whatever your concerns are, find a polite, concise way to state them. They will be grateful to you for your honesty and invariably will respect you for it.

If you're confident in your answer and they really want you, they might actually offer you something better. Who knows? Stranger things have happened, and this occurs more often than you might think. It all depends on how you have handled the interview process and the negotiations with them. It also depends on the quality of the relationship/cultural fit you have established with the decision-makers, and the degree of trust you have shown throughout the hiring process. Don't second-guess anything. Just lay your cards on the table, politely and clearly. Authenticity always rules!

> *I stayed stuck for too long. I could have saved myself two or three years by making decisions sooner. That would be the thing I would change more than anything: Having the confidence to make the needed changes, when you recognize that things are not working and it's time to move on. Life's too short.*

—Michael Leclair, partner
www.spacetigers.info

3.4 COUNTER-OFFERS

Finally, in some instances, **your current employer may make a counter-offer** when you hand in your notice. While belatedly appreciated, counter-offers seldom work out. They promise you something, and you turn down the other job. Then, their promises either don't materialize or, when they do, they are less, lower, or slower than you expected.

If it's the case where they actually offer you what you want and deserve, and you like the company, it is up to you to accept it. **However, get the offer in writing before you turn down the new offer.** You can always find a creative excuse to "stall" a new offer for twenty-four-to-forty-eight hours (but no more). If your company really wants you to stay, HR can make it happen within forty-eight hours. Make forty-eight hours a "hard boundary". If they don't honour it, take that as a (not-so-positive) sign, and take the opportunity to re-evaluate their commitment to you.

If you move forward with the counter-offer, create an exit statement to get out of the new offer. You guessed it: Take your former "business case" ("why you" "why now" "why this role" "why this company") statement and amend it to state (on reflection) what isn't working for you . . . and . . . stick to it like glue.

All of the above = managing your message.

And you'd be doing it right!

Well done!

> ❝ *I think the biggest mistake is not trusting your own judgement. It can be quite easy for your boss to direct your activities and career choices, to funnel you down a particular avenue and make suggestions*

for you. But are they doing this with your best interests in mind? People will try to influence you for their own interests. Step back, and ask yourself if this is the best thing to do—to make a move or not, to take on a particular piece of work or not. Give yourself the opportunity to make your own decisions."

—Andy Robling, vice-president, client development
www.hays.com

It really is all about you.

.

CHAPTER 18

HOW TO START YOUR NEW JOB ON THE RIGHT FOOT

Congratulations! You have executed a successful job search and have secured an offer from the company of your (current) dreams. Now the journey begins! To quote my dear friend and colleague Karen Young, "Please be aware that it takes more than buying a new outfit and finding a new coffee shop on the way to work!"

Critical to the new role are:

1. An accurate/acceptable job title; and

2. Fair market value in terms of compensation.

Start with the right mix.

Logistics: Anxiety and excitement are all part of the process. Prior to joining, it is useful to **clarify details with your direct report to ensure a smooth entry** that will help establish trust and organizational ability. This includes: Start and quit times, location for your office space/desk, dress code, security details, HR forms/processes, social media rules, etc. It is vital that your new employer's expectations are met. It is equally vital for you to divulge your needs: If you need to be out at five for daycare once a week but can start early to compensate, be up front and ask about it. Similarly, if you need the second Friday of every month for a specific commitment, discuss it, and plan for it. All the foregoing will speak to your organizational skills and your wish to fit in smoothly from the start, and will set your future colleagues up for success while you're at it.

MINDSET ALERT! A new gig is exciting, to be sure. But you must wrap your head around the fact that, yes, there's a lot of positive potential here, but **there are also going to be negative aspects that evolve over time**. How you handle them will speak directly to the kind of professional you are. You need to have *realistic expectations* of the role you are going to play, as well as how your co-workers will handle themselves, and how the company handles itself. When things go wrong, it is no time to regress to your twenties and silently suffer "workplace reality shock." Hence, the need to research the company before taking the job—*this is your responsibility and your best insurance policy for not landing in a nightmare job.*

> " *Get knowledge and experience with new media skills. Always be learning. The future is digital; know how to best utilize various online platforms and stay up to date on trends and new technology. Be flexible. Don't always play it safe. Challenge traditional models, but remember some things never change: you can't lose with a positive attitude and strong worth ethic. Be the leader in the room.* "

—Hudson Mack, veteran news director and anchor
www.harbourpublishing.com/title/HudsonMack

Music to my ears: "Be the leader in the room."

On Day One, your new boss should take the opportunity to give you a briefing on your new role vis-à-vis the company's expectations. It's a super-smart move to go in with an **entry strategy** of your own that outlines/clarifies your short-term (three-month) and long-term (twelve-month) priorities. Then, **confirm those priorities in an informal email.** Your entry strategy will cover you in case the job spec changes mid-stream, or when they change their expectations of your role but neglect to formalize it with you. This can and does happen.

Onboarding & Key Performance Indicators (KPIs): The job description will have provided an outline of the key responsibility areas that you can begin addressing. Companies will have varying processes for onboarding—if they are weak in this area, there is a lot you can do to onboard yourself: Ask if the company has an operations manual, review key files shared on the company's intranet, read through the annual report, study the production schedule and their product/services, study their marketing practices, read their recent news releases, and/or review the competition. There is much you can do to raise your confidence level and set yourself up for a successful onboarding.

Meeting the Team: When introduced to new colleagues, keep the discussions relatively social in nature. **Always be welcoming and inclusive to everyone.** Keep the introductions brief. Make a point of committing their first names to memory (and use them). Close by asking if you might call at a later time to set a meeting to better acquaint yourselves and debrief on shared areas of responsibility. These new relationships are critical to your success over the long term, and it is a strategic advantage to start forging strong, reciprocal relationships from the onset. Take the initiative and set your new colleagues up for success. They'll appreciate the courtesy.

First impressions are critically important. The very first thing you say, and the circumstances in which you present (aka context) are the ones that are going to stick with your colleagues—this is no time to be too comfortable! If you're unsure about your management style, consider working with a business coach or mentor to help raise awareness of your strengths and weaknesses. Put your best *feet* forward. Professionalism, compassion, humour, patience, and respect are all good attributes to bring to the table—and not just on the first day . . . you must sustain them. Make "staying in charge of your own message" a true *hallmark* of your professional game.

More Mindset Advice! The political climate is going to be a fact. Absorb the history, understand the present, and stay mindful of the future. Learn about the culture and adjust to it. Stick to business. Ongoing cultural and political fit is mission-critical. *Over the long term, incremental gains are greater than overnight sensations.* They are not necessarily looking for a superstar—they just want good, strong performers who can display leadership and professionalism in their individual areas. Most importantly, they want teammates who fit in, and contribute reliably and consistently to the organization's mandate, values, and ultimately, its' bottom line. Be this person.

A great book to read: *The Secret Handshake: Mastering The Politics of The Business Inner Circle*, by Kathleen Kelly Reardon. I read it back in 2002 and actually found this book to be life changing. Her advice truly stands the test of time today.

> **"**In my earlier years, I was always rushing toward change because it was possible. And I think that's where people still make a lot of mistakes. Most established companies have their own cultures and methods, and better reasons for retaining them than an industry newcomer suspects. Claims of necessary disruption are really hyped. There are some exceptions, but they are not the rule. Mostly things happen incrementally—you have to have patience. There's a far more strategic, sustainable approach: work with the team you've got. Understand why things are done in a certain way, and understand your systems. Mistakes tend to get made by blowing things up or disrupting the business—where, in fact, you just really need to fine-tune existing systems.**"**

—Kirk LaPointe, editor-in-chief
www.biv.com, www.kirklapointe.ca

What about the bad apple on the team? There's always something . . . or someone! Internally, I encourage you to practice empathy for the team member who just can't get it together, and try to help where you can. If you don't know how to maintain *healthy boundaries*, now's the time to learn. Set the example for others and treat this person with compassion, respect and professional courtesy. Take the high road. Maintain decent boundaries. Don't get personal. Cut the person a decent and humane amount of slack. *Be sure to reinforce and/or reward this person when they do things right.* Compassion is key.

★ Professional jealousy, oppositional defiance, feeling threatened, a hot temper, gossip, and/or an attitude of superiority (or resentment), are the kisses of death. Commit to dropping any competitive attitude at the door, every day that you walk through it.

During the first few weeks with the company, it is helpful to be a "professional observer", by taking the time to get to know all stakeholders, agendas and issues. Commit yourself to being a contributing team member. Everyone has a role—and everyone should be respected for it. Be sure you learn how to toe the party line, and toe it.

MORE MINDSET ADVICE: Perspective is everything, so please take the long view. It is commonly accepted that it takes three weeks to get the lay of the land in an organization, six weeks to start to feel comfortable, and twelve weeks to feel truly settled. During the initial weeks, it is prudent not to make judgments, assumptions, or suggestions on any one topic, unless you have taken the opportunity to hear the entire team and its' issues out. At three months, you should know all the players, have a decent comfort level with them, know how to get things accomplished, and be ready to take more of a leadership role in internal initiatives. With the proper groundwork done, the road should be paved for a relatively smooth and successful first year, establishing both your relationships and track record, and providing the opportunity to create some successes that you can build on over the longer-term . . . not to mention earn that cost-of-living increase (and performance bonus) next year!

Bon courage!

CHAPTER 19

RECRUITING REALITIES

A primer on differing talents' needs, and how to help them help themselves with "Career Activism" strategies . . .

Emerging/Graduating Talent: Need to learn how to market themselves properly by building and managing their brand. They need professional exposure in order to develop their business knowledge. They should be actively encouraged to build soft skills. They need the direct, *hands-on* assistance of their school career and/or alumni departments to help them obtain internships. Family and extended family can help by providing introductions and referrals. Emerging talent need mentors—especially mentors with solid business experience, like boomers! Finally, they need to actively network and build their connections. Give them a hand-up. Or give them a job. Make a point of making a targeted introduction for emerging talent. Help them find networking gigs and show them how to successfully network in real time.

Gen Z/iGen: Need up-to-date marketing materials and a bona-fide methodology for accessing the hidden job market (refer to Chapter 12's "The Hidden Job Market"). They need to learn *when not to apply for a job* (refer to Chapter 15's "Can You

Make the Shortlist?") and how to make a business case for any candidacy they pursue (pretty sure this is covered ad nauseam throughout this book). In short, they need to know how to capture HR's favourable attention. They need to learn how to approach decision-makers effectively—by *scripting* and *rehearsing* their approaches. They are well advised to practice these pitches on the companies they care the least about, before taking a run at the companies they care the most about. Last, they need business coaches and mentors . . . and regular networking.

Mid-career talent/Gens X, Y, Z: Need to be able to clearly state their role and value in the marketplace; they need to understand their actual worth, and need to be able to articulate that worth properly for advancement. They also need ongoing professional development and opportunities to build their business acumen (mentors, joining working groups, etc.), and should be actively building their *business knowledge*, *business vocabulary*, and *skills base*. They need to maintain a serious focus on managing their contacts and building and leveraging their networks. In order to understand where the markets are going, it is recommended that they read the annual or bi-annual industry forecasts of the world's largest business management firms – there are many, and many of them still, are sector specific. *These business reports forecast where various industries are headed, which also foreshadow where the jobs are likely to be.*

Career Transition/Boomers: Boomers need trustworthy, committed "learning partners" they can turn to, to share their issues with, and to discuss and develop business leads. In many cases, they need to build freelance and entrepreneurial skills to be able to participate in the gig economy. They need to monetize a skill or hobby and/or develop a consultancy in their area of expertise. Or both. They also need to build their marketing tools, and be able market their skills and knowledge over multiple platforms. They could stand to hang with Gens X, Y, and Z, and learn about technology trends and social-media marketing. They don't have to learn the technology, but they should definitely be aware of various platforms' strengths and capabilities and maintain a steady presence on one or two social media platforms to promote their hobby or business/consultancies.

International students and new Canadians need a broad picture of, and induction to, the Canadian labour markets, as well as an understanding of the soft skills required to network successfully in Canada. They need to be guided in how and where to find the companies, trade associations, chambers of commerce and/or thought leaders in their professional field—joining or being introduced to professional networking groups will serve them exceptionally well. They need to learn how to strategically plan positive "marketing touchdowns" (refer to Chapter 12's "The Hidden Job Market") with would-be employers, to help gain their trust, build relationships, and secure a job, and/or critical employment sponsorships.

Job seekers in all groups need positive reinforcement from friends, family, and peers. They don't need to have their confidence undermined, nor do they need to be second-guessed on their job search efforts, their choices and/or their goals. They are doing the best that they can. Support them! Because . . . if you are not part of the solution, you are definitely part of the problem.

Job seekers in all groups also need to learn the basics of entrepreneurship, and how to *build*, *market*, and *run* their own small businesses. Note: mediaINTELLIGENCE has a presentation online on the Career Toolkit page, which offers "Smart Start: How to Start Your own Small Business." Click here and scroll to bottom: http://www.mediaintelligence.ca/estore-career-toolkit/

Everyone can truly help by paying it forward for others. If you consider your social circle for just a few minutes, it won't take any time at all to think of a friend, colleague, or family member who is struggling with un/under-employment. If you're secure in a job, pay it forward for someone else by reaching out and facilitating their efforts. Everyone needs help, true support, and affirmation. Who in your circle needs help right now? Write yourself a note in your weekly schedule planning, to reach out to them and offer them a hand-up in any way that you can.

Life-long learning: For anyone looking to broaden their skills, build some "street creds" by taking short webinars, seminars, listening to podcasts, and/or attending conferences. These small "c" credentials can be added to both your resume content and LinkedIn profile. Make it a point to incorporate life-long learning into your professional activities whenever and wherever possible.

❝ *I would say get closer to analytics sooner. People are saying that data are the new oil. It might be a bit of an over-reaching cliché, or maybe not. When you look at the formidable change that's happening under the umbrella of AI, new automation, and machine learning—all driven by data—we have to learn to work with it and understand it. I've certainly invested a fair amount of time in the last five years [in these areas]. Had I done that earlier, I'd be that much more ahead of the game. Or maybe more in the game!* **❞**

—Glenn O'Farrell, président et chef de la direction
  www.groupemediatfo.org

CHAPTER 20

THE LONG VIEW

What would you do if I asked you to sit still in a chair for fifteen minutes and do nothing, with no personal devices allowed? At best, you would probably feel highly uncomfortable. At worst, you would probably covertly or overtly panic. Most people cannot last two minutes (let alone fifteen) simply being, and doing nothing.

Which brings us to self-awareness and self-care.

> ❝ *You need to adopt two attitudes: learning all the time, and developing a greater understanding of yourself, and others. Don't assume that you're ever going to get out of continuing education, and don't make the classic error that you can ride any wealth of experience for any extended period of time. Learn, all the time! And you'll need to have a greater self-awareness: spend time getting to understand different cultures, histories and systems. As functions become more automated, the human factor will become*

increasingly important. You can effectively contribute by having a higher degree of empathy, compassion, respect and understanding."

——Kirk LaPointe, editor-in-chief
www.biv.com, www.kirklapointe.ca

You need to establish balance and boundaries between your professional and personal lives. You cannot be a truly effective professional *or* human, if you are putting in twelve- or fourteen-hour days, twenty-four/seven. At least not indefinitely—though it may work for you for a while. You need to establish balance between your professional and personal lives. Eight a.m. to six p.m., give it your all. After that, give it as little as possible. If you must work at night, draft up your emails and/or proposals, review them in the morning, and "hit send" at nine a.m. the next business day. For heavens' sakes ★ don't send the message that you are willing to work around the clock. ★ Don't send emails on weekends. ★ Don't rely on "texts" for your business correspondence. These are all considered to be bad form. Establish some healthy boundaries, and maintain them. By which I mean . . .

You need to practice self-care, *especially* in job search. The latest report at this writing, is that job search in Canada takes an average of twenty-seven weeks. There are some days when you will power-out and be as efficient as can be. There will be other days when all you will be able to manage is to "turn the plants on the window sill." You need to allow yourself a break from job search, and recognize when you just don't have it in you to perform at top standard. Allow yourself some breathing space.

Put a hard focus on your physical and emotional health. Maintain clear and effective boundaries. You are in charge of the rules of your life: So take the opportunity to identify where you can afford to let go, and where you would benefit from setting tougher boundaries. Give your "life rules" some fresh thought, and don't let anyone or any industry run you into the ground. Learn to take care of yourself *first*. When push comes to shove, you will learn that you are *much* more important than the company whose call you are waiting on.

Learn to fortify yourself. Face your mistakes, know your shortcomings, and accept (or conquer) them. Build your knowledge, your capacity, and "agency"—aka "the capacity of exerting power." Take your supplements and mind your nutrition, as well as your mental health. Get some air and exercise. Learn to breathe properly. Socialize for non-professional reasons. Focus on the greater good, *always* . . .and how you can contribute to it. In other words, be sure to replenish your own well.

Learn to check out. In each and every one of my days, I build in *balance breaks*, usually at lunch, when I leave my desk and mentally check out for half an hour, and at five p.m., when I take an hour to myself and just enjoy my dog. I also take one *full* day off each week. Religiously. You don't have to learn to meditate (although it would certainly be to your benefit to build that practice), you just need to learn to stop. Stop everything. Stop for a few minutes. Quiet your mind. It's a lot easier said than done, but do develop and practice the skill. Ground yourself daily by getting out into the sun and fresh air. Give yourself permission to check out. If you don't master balance, you are setting yourself up for chronic disease and/or dysfunction later in life. Your precious life and soul deserve more than this.

Take "checking out" one step further, and learn to put your own oxygen mask on first. Learn to say no! If you are uncomfortable saying no to something, by all means, use your career coach (that would be me) as an excuse. As in: "I am unable to attend the [baby shower] [family dinner] [charity golf tournament] as I have an assignment to work on [x] for my career coach." (I don't mind being the bad guy at all. Blame it on me.)

> **"** Keep reading books that try to narrate the changing circumstances of the shifts in our economy. The operating system of our world is changing—the system that governed our lives, work, social circumstances, and academics. That operating order/system is shifting to a new one. And it's going to continue to become even more different with blockchain, disintermediation, and economic transitions of the future unfolding in every way. There's going to be a lot more disruption. We see sparks of genius on every horizon!**"**

—Glenn O'Farrell, président et chef de la direction
www.groupemediatfo.org

Build your self-esteem: A number of years ago (probably mid-career, when I was struggling with under-employment), a mentor suggested that I **write up an "accomplishments list"**. She suggested that I write a full list of every.single.thing that I had accomplished, in each year of my life, since I left home. Whatever I felt to be a personal accomplishment, I was to put on that list. So one day, I took the time to write it up. Then she told me to average out the list by adding up all the accomplishments and dividing them by the total number of years I had been out on my own. *The results were staggering! It was a truly revelatory exercise.* When complete, there was absolutely no doubt remaining in my mind about my capacity to deliver on my own goals. And there was no downplaying the sheer volume of successes that I had previously not given much thought or any credit to. I suspect the same will happen for you if you write up your accomplishments list. Your self-esteem will automatically increase and will have a long-lasting impact on your view of yourself—aka give yourself some credit, already!

Build your resilience: The most critical aspects of building resilience are: to a) work on developing a truly positive mindset; and b) work on *accepting* and *adjusting* to change (or loss of any sort). Watch your reactions to change and avoid over-inflating, or 'crisis-creating" in any given situation. Understand that you will make mistakes. Own them. Share the coping skills you have learned with others. The society we live in is much more competitive than it is nurturing. So learn to nurture yourself with self-care, compassion, mindful contemplation, and acceptance. Keep your best interests and thoughts at the forefront of everything. Stick to them like glue. Make them your new way of life, and strengthen them each year in your goals list.

Maintain a consistent focus on what you want and need. This will take care of itself if you just do your birthday homework! I cannot stress enough how taking active steps to manage your goals and taking care of your career homework will benefit you over the long term. Being prepared, informed, rehearsed, and targeted will make you so much more successful because it will put you in front of the process (read: proactive and in charge), rather than playing catch-up from behind (read:

reactive to marketplace—throwing stuff at the wall, hoping something sticks). Maintaining your focus and taking proactive steps will also substantially increase your income over your lifespan. Think about that! Write up your annual goals, scrub your marketing pieces, work your "job search research/contacts database," and rehearse your scripts. In other words, practice career activism!

Learn to be your own BFF. You owe it to your best self: be this person! Gift yourself with self-actualization—on your terms. Your career is in your hands. All you really have to do is hold up your end.

You can be in charge of your career, or you can be reactive to it.

Your call.

ACKNOWLEDGEMENTS

I owe each of these friends and colleagues a tremendous debt of gratitude for their trust and support throughout the years. Each person and organization acknowledged here has directly or indirectly contributed to the career success of the thousands who have graced mediaINTELLIGENCE's doors throughout our fifteen years of recruiting and coaching in media:

Neishaw Ali, Academy of Canadian Cinema and Television, Algonquin College, Don Bastien, Lisa Batke, Towa Beer, Mrs. Bell, M'sieu Jacques Bensimon, Barbara Bowlby, Broadcast Dialogue, Alexandra Brown, Fredelle Brief, Jamie Brown, Grant Buchanan, Jim Byrd, Martin Byrne, Deanna Cadette, Joe Cameron, Alisyn Camerota, Canadian Association of Broadcasters, Canadian Media Producers' Association, Adriana Carlin, Suzanne Carpenter, John Cassaday, Sally Catto, Joe Chan, Shan Chandrasekar, Centennial College, Chanda Chevannes, Susan Cohen, Catherine Copelin, Amy Cowan, Sarah Crawford, Alan Cross, Marni DeKerkhove, Christa Dickenson, Mark Dillon, Pam Dinsmore, Elizabeth Duffy-McLean, Deluxe Films, Kadon Douglas, Durham College, Terry Edmunds, Jeffrey Elliott, Brian Ellis, Film Training Manitoba, Heather Findlay, Renée Gluck, Mme. Suzanne Gouin, M'sieu Alain Gourd, Peter Grant, Richard Grey, Tom Haberstroh, Jacky Habib, Annie Hadida, Mark Hand, Peter Herrndorf, Hot

Docs, John Hudecki, Rae Hull, Humber College, IQ Partners, Adam Ivers, Tara Jan, Huguette Jean, Mister Donald Johnson, Wendy Jones, Richard Kavanagh, Linda Kerec, Raja Khanna, Gloria Ui Young Kim, Tanya Kelen, David Kincaid, David Kines, Caroline Konrad, Jenn Kuzmyk, Monique Lafontaine, Lucie Lalumiere, Robert Lantos, Kirk LaPointe, Jean LaRose, Michael Leclair, Karen Lee, Claude Lemieux, Slava Levin, John Lewis, Paul Lewis, Mauro Lollo, Wally Longul, Loyalist College, Peter Lyman, Lisa Lyons, Jim Macdonald, Hudson Mack, Mark Marren, Monique McCallister, Gavin McGarry, Dan McLellan, Catherine McLeod, Donna Messer, Craig Moffitt, Mohawk College, Robert Montgomery, Jennifer Mossop, Bill Mustos, Ken Murphy, Rose Nadon, Desrine Nelson, Susan Nobel, Jacqueline Nuwame, Francesca O'Brien, Greg O'Brien, Glenn O'Farrell, Kevin O'Keefe, Mike Omelus, David Onley, John Panikkar, Richard Patterson, Brad Phillips, Playback Magazine, Dave Pong, Jack Ponte, Ross Porter, Mary Powers, Mark Prasuhn, Frank Pulumbarit, Lally Rementilla, Daniel Richler, Bill Roberts, Kristian Roberts, Kathryn Robinson, Andy Robling, Harvey Rodgers, Ryerson University, Kathy Ross, Susan Ross, Kevin Shea, Patricia Scarlett, Sheridan Scott, Christine Sharp-Fox, Peggy Shkuda, Michael Steinberg, Stephen Stohn, Gayle Swann, Jay Switzer, HRH Maggie Stratton, Cynthia Taylor, Michael Taylor, Dennie Theodore, Chuck Thompson, Pierre Touchette, Women in Film and Television—Toronto, Peter Vamos, Gervais Vignola, Paula Virany, Colette Vosberg-Johnson, Louise Wallace, Catherine Warren, Colette Watson, Danny Webber, Mrs. Wilcox, Kate Wood, Braden Wright, York University, and Tandy Yull.

Special thanks go to **Mikhial Gurarie** for his oh-so-diligent tech support, and infinite good humour. Special mention also goes to **Karen Young** for her ongoing enthusiasm of all things ml, as well as her leadership and longstanding commitment to emerging talent.

Finally, greatest thanks to my inspiration and muse, **Mary Dwyer-Nadon.** Mary taught me how to get in the ring and fight. She also encouraged me to have a good time doing it. Her formidable voice rings through the ages to the pages of this book.

Each of these individuals affirmed and encouraged me to take risks, and honour my chosen path. Eventually my purpose was set and my confidence grew. From there, and with time, I was able to advance my own subject-matter-expertise and stake my claim in my desired profession.

It's been such a cool, inspiring and satisfying journey—all made so much easier, fun and enriching by all these precious friends and colleagues.

Amitiés, mitch avec stella.

CPSIA information can be obtained
at www.ICGtesting.com
Printed in the USA
LVHW041522170419
614525LV00002B/214